LIBRARY OF THE ARTS

THE LANGUAGE OF CLASSICAL BALLET

Flavia Pappacena

The Language of Classical Ballet

Guide to the Interpretation of Iconographic Sources

ENGLISH TRANSLATION
BY BRUCE MICHELSON

LIBRARY OF THE ARTS
Texts and study tools for school and university
Dance Section directed by Flavia Pappacena

Original Title:
Il linguaggio della danza classica
(Gremese © 2012)

Cover Design:
Patrizia Marroco

Cover Photo:
Costume sketch by Caramba for the allegory *Concord*, from the 1908-09 La Scala production of the *gran ballo Excelsior*. From the collection of the Fondazione Cassa di Risparmio di Alessandria.

Photocomposition:
emMeCiPi – Rome

Printed in China

to my Husband

Table of Contents

Introduction

Since the 1700s, all of the authors writing about dance from a theoretic or historical viewpoint have underlined the centrality of both the visual component in choreographic performance and, more generally, the visual messages contained within the dancer's movements. Many of these texts, particularly those of a didactic nature, present a wealth of illustrations that, although originally intended to help visualize academic principles and render the concepts more incisive, nevertheless also stand as testimony to the steadily growing function of the image as an instrument of instruction. While our ability to trace the principal aesthetics and communicative logic of the 18th and 19th Centuries is due, above all, to the existence of didactic manuals, other iconographic sources grant us proximity to the general aesthetics and function of choreographic performance. Historiographical publications on dance and research papers published in professional journals and presented at international conferences have restituted an array of images (costume sketches, scenic designs, illustrations of events, portraits), from which a considerable number of cognitive elements about dance in the 1700s and 1800s has emerged.

In 1795, when new uniforms for those carrying out public office were planned by the Directory, the Abbot Grégoire wrote: "The language of signs possesses its own eloquence: distinctive costumes are part of this idiom, that is, they reveal ideas and sentiments analogous to their object"; and this is yet more true for the ballet. Costume sketches, particularly those from the 1700s, for example, represent an invaluable source of documentation, revealing the attributes of characters and sometimes their manner of dancing, as well, which can be reconstructed from the fashioning and ornamentation, but also from the figures' attitudes, which, in many cases, are reproduced with great accuracy.

Under careful examination, costumes sketches also reveal other essential functions assigned to the costume, among these, the capacity to transmit complex concepts, utilizing the symbology with which the visual culture of the period was impregnated.

Among the sources of iconographic material worthy of note are certain manuscripts of choreographic transcriptions, the graphic formulation of which is strongly oriented toward visual comprehension. These, too, reveal a string of revelatory information about techniques – regarding both composition and execution – and the dynamic relation between aesthetic thought and production.

The purpose of this book is to offer an illustrative sampling from diverse iconographic sources, accompanying this with indications to help guide the reader toward a correct interpretation of these images and, through this, to an analysis of the aesthetic and technical fundaments of dance. While the limits of space have imposed upon the selection of images and compelled its containment within the terms conventionally regarded as the "historical" phase of classical ballet – from the *ballet de cour* through to late 19th-Century dance – the choice to follow a concise conceptual path, rather than one of comprehensive documentation, has led to the

inevitable omission of certain moments of historical import, such as the artistic adventures of August Bournonville.
The sampling presented reflects sources relevant to the creation, production, preservation, theory and didactics of ballet, and it favors certain central themes that have remained insufficiently analyzed and discussed, specifically: the inspiration provided by classical iconography, the influence of fashion, the persistence of tradition, the functions of scenery and costumes, and the performing space itself.
In order to explain visually how deeply rooted dance has been to the culture of the day, as well as the complexity of its connections and links to other cultural domains, images from various source types (figurative arts, applied arts, traditional costumes) have been juxtaposed alongside terpsichorean images, and the images chosen are those in which the sharing of iconographic schemes or the exchange of symbolic messages between dance and society is most clearly revealed.

Flavia Pappacena
October, 2011

From *Ballet de Cour* to the Affirmation of Dance as an Autonomous Art Form

It would not be possible to approach the diversity of expressive forms in French ballet during the 18th and 19th Centuries without first taking a look at the magnificent performances and innovations in lyric theater brought about by Louis XIV.
The *ballet de cour*, or court ballet, the first example of which was the *Ballet comique de la Reine* (1581), was a grandiose type of performance, conceived as an ideal encounter of the arts of poetry, music, dance and painting, for the solemn glorification of the Sovereign. Its various sections alternated between recitation, song, instrumental music and dance; and these were filled with a variegated multitude of characters, in some cases interpreted by the court nobles themselves, including the king and members of the royal family.
These characters belonged to a variety of settings: from the world of classical mythology (major and minor divinities, nymphs, fauns, etc.) to that of allegory, including fantastical figures from the theater of antiquity, but also realistic characters representative of the various trades or belonging to assorted nationalities. Titles such as *Ballet des Saisons* or *Le Triomphe de l'Amour* highlight how a plot could, in fact, serve as a pretext for a magnificent and sumptuous allegory, rich with striking scenic effects and picturesque costumes in the style desired by Louis XIV and subject to the norms that he imposed on all of the arts.
Also to be considered in the category of grand performances are the royal feasts, which often extended over some days and included various types of entertainment and theatrical performances. For dance, these occasions offered increased visibility, as well as further opportunities for the tangible confirmation of the high esteem in which it was held at the royal courts, and above all, by the "Sun King" himself.
The importance of dance and its recognition by official French culture, through the codified models of *ballet de cour*, was to profoundly influence the reform of French musical theater, to the point that performances of both the new form of opera – the *tragédie lyrique*, created by Jean-Baptiste Lully in 1673 – and the new *opéra-ballet*, born just a few years later in 1695, would have dances and academic ballets distributed throughout (in all the acts and immediately following the prologue), performed by professional (male) dancers and, in growing numbers, by female dancers, as well.
Such ballets were inserted as an integral component into the fabric of opera theater and *opéra-ballets*, despite the fact that the dancers were not granted roles within the dramatic development of the action, but rather were secondary and "filling" figures – followers of the divinities or members of a king's court, for example, or inhabitants of the place where the action was set. These supporting roles were often quite important to the context (the grape harvesters, for example, in a scene set at the end of the vintage). These characters had their faces covered by showy masks, and they moved using an intricate *terre-à-terre* technique, with which they sculpted spatial trajectories that were formulated on rigorous geometrical designs.
These dances provided for the participation of a number of dancers, but most often, they consisted principally of *pas de deux*, *pas de trois* and solos, all of high technical

standards. Combined with the splendor of the costumes and masks, they resulted in highly spectacular effects.
The structure of the ballets within the operas and *opéra-ballets*, based on symmetrical choreographic designs and executed by masked dancers, would remain unaltered until nearly the end of the Louis XV's reign, that is, into the early 1770s. And it was precisely this lack of change that pushed French academic dance toward a technical virtuosity that became more and more ostentatious, although still remaining within the codified norms of the Académie Royale de Danse and the rules dictated by the tastes of the dominant class, that is, the aristocracy.
The abolition of masks and the decline of *opéra-ballet* and symmetrical academic ballets were strictly connected to the affirmation across Europe of a new form of ballet with a narrative structure, which was called the *ballet d'action* or *ballet pantomime*.
Although these ballets of a narrative structure that were causing such a sensation first appeared in the early 1760s (staged by Jean-Georges Noverre in Stuttgart and Gaspero Angiolini in Vienna), the origins of this form can be traced back to experimentation carried out by certain artists in various European cities, beginning as early as the 1730s and -40s, or even to some sporadic experiments in the 1710s (by John Weaver in London and Claude Ballon with Françoise Prévost at the court in Sceaux). As much as these experiments were ascribable to a variety of aesthetic lines, they were also all connected in one way or another to a movement toward classicist restoration that had begun to make important inroads, carried along by a wave of "rediscovery" of the theater of antiquity, or later, as a response to the excesses of Rococo. In some cases, these experiments bore the signs of influence or contamination by dramatic theater or the actors who were heirs to the Commedia dell'Arte, or by the acrobats of Italian *grotesque* dance; but in large part, they were the results of a forceful attraction to painting, which, in Enlightenment thought, was considered a sister art to dance, together with poetry and music. All of these experiments aimed to stimulate public satisfaction through the beauty of the performance itself and through interest for the way in which the subject was treated. They took place in a diversity of theaters: from the Opéra-Comique (for example, Noverre in 1750s) to the Comédie-Française (Jean-Baptiste De Hesse, for example), or in other playhouses, and then in the Paris Opera and other official theaters in the great European capitals: Vienna, Stuttgart and St. Petersburg, et al.
As in classical theater, the structure of narrative ballets developed according to the canonic tri-partitioning: description/action/development, alternating between stage movement, pantomime set to music, and passages of pure dance. In all its parts, the ballet, following 18th-Century custom, made use of complex scenic vehicles to become a grandiose spectacle. The ballets by Jean-Georges Noverre (1727-1810), in particular, were conceived as large, composite 'frescoes', in which the oft-recurring danced sections were interwoven with group actions, creating movement that was as spatially complex as it was structurally unified and stylistically homogeneous. Such danced sections were inserted into the dramatic fabric in various ways, and they contributed to the creation of a masterly balance between visual pleasure and the deep emotional involvement of the public. These were the novelties that, together with the publication in 1760 of his theoretic *Lettres sur la Danse et sur les Ballets*, turned Noverre into the figure most representative of the process of rebuilding dance

theater that was to affect Europe between the mid-century and the 1760s and -70s. Observing the situation in Europe around the mid-1700s in its totality, a notable variety of plot subjects can be discerned; and one also gathers a basic difference in the selection of sources of inspiration, which could range from the tragic theater of antiquity to theatrical literature from the 1600s (above all, French), but also included various myths and poems. Franz Anton Hilverding (1710-1768), for instance, was inspired by Racine's *Britannicus*; Gaspero Angiolini (1731-1803) drew from Molière for his *Dom Juan ou le Festin de pierre* and from Voltaire for his ballets *Sémiramis* and *L'Orphelin de la Chine*. Noverre, on the other hand, even though attracted by ancient tragic theater, loved above all to translate into ballet the adventures narrated in classical mythology and epic poetry. Among these were *Renaud et Armide* (from *Gerusalemme liberata* [Jerusalem Delivered] by Torquato Tasso), *Énée et Didon* (from the *Aeneid*) and *La Descente d'Orphée aux Enfers* (from Ovid's *Metamorphoses*). Noverre also used comic plots and lively comedies situated in rural settings. Comic plots in peasant settings, present in ballets during the 1760s, but as a minority, became a trend during the few short years of Louis XVI's reign (1775-1789). Crafty maidens who trick their mothers in stories that were immersed in the peasant frameworks typical of the joyous comedies created for the Opéra-Comique provided a pretext for talented choreographers, such as Maximilien Gardel (*La Chercheuse d'esprit*, *Ninette à la cour*, Paris Opera, 1778) and Dauberval (*La Fille mal gardée*, Bordeaux, 1789). But the choreographers were also attracted by a certain "Spanish" thread. Noverre created one ballet entitled *Don Quixote*, and Jean-Baptiste Blache and Dauberval staged ballets inspired by *The Barber of Seville* and Beaumarchais' *The Marriage of Figaro*.

It was, however, the influence of both Neoclassicism and Greek fashion, stirred up by the digs at Herculaneum and Pompeii (begun in 1738 and 1748, respectively), that would stimulate the greatest technical innovations and constitute the main thread in ballets of the late 1700s and early 1800s. While Pierre Gardel (1758-1840) staged the ballets *Psyché*, *Télémaque dans l'île de Calypso* and *Le Jugement de Pâris* at the Paris Opera – all inspired by profound moral themes – the Dionysian vision from the world of antiquity rediscovered through the archaeological digs, was spurring a process of regeneration of the basic principles of academic dance that, while not impairing the normative system of the Académie Royale de Danse, did however oppose it with provocative transgressions in style and technique. Such transgressions, which Noverre would define with a scornful tone as *arabesques*, were inspired by the extravagance and unreality typical of the *grotesque* decorations from Raphaelian tradition, in which the same concept of *arabesque* in painting as in dance can be identified. We encounter here a fascinating contradiction between the negation of the entire basis of the imitative arts – the principle of the imitation of nature – and the exaltation of "ideal beauty", revisited with a modern sensitivity; but we also see a new sensitivity as regards irrational and fantastical elements, an early portent of Romantic ballet.

The contamination, however, was much more widespread, and this was deeply connected to aesthetic changes and political and social upheaval. Costumes, too, were to be subverted, as would dance technique and the relationship between men's and women's dancing; the French Revolution and the arrival of the new century were indeed to open the doors definitively to a new way of dancing.

In the first half of the 19th Century, the numerous innovations that had gradually affected stage design and stage technology reverted onto ballet. Following the great mobility gained through the advent of the drop-curtain, which eliminated the need for visible scene changes, gas illumination was introduced in 1822, resulting in the substitution of high-hanging chandeliers and favoring a more articulate and functional use of light. Stage design would also gradually adjust its spatial orientation, as painted wings were replaced with architectural elements and furnishings. Also important – although with different objectives – were the "practicables" and the mechanical devices that would allow apparitions to appear from below the stage and the miraculous raising and lowering of people and objects. The subjects of these actions were, however, no longer Pluto and Proserpina, or Mercury, messenger of the Olympian deities; or Medea's carriage, rising toward the sky, followed by monsters; but rather, it was the Zephyrs, Elves and Sylphides that did the flying in the new Romantic ballet.
The arrival of the 19th Century was also characterized by a new heterogeneity as regards thematic choices and the experimentation with diverse settings. While progress in the sciences and medicine would provide new potential for analyzing the body and exploring movement, the nascent "physical education" would impose upon dance the adjustment of its educative mission, widening the scope of educational programs for amateurs. Operations to revise and systemize didactic methodology closely mirrored the developments in technique, which, shaking off the weight of conditioning and prejudice, opened up to wider and freer horizons. Women's dancing gained a more visible platform as regards technique and began to specialize in an innovative way in the *terre-à-terre* form, and by the late 1820s, the acrobatic technique of rising to the extreme tips of the toes had already been conquered, lending itself to a variety of uses, depending on the ballet's plot: from displays of bravura and virtuosity, to the illusion of a ballerina's weightlessness. The founding of the ballet schools at La Scala in Milan (1813) and the San Carlo Theater in Naples (1812), both initially directed by artists from the Paris Opera, contributed to the widespread diffusion of French dance in Italy and brought home artists like Carlo Blasis, who, having trained in France, was to lift the Milanese school to the heights of international fame. Similar cases of foreign artists who had studied and performed at the Paris Opera occurred in other countries: in Denmark, for example, which would see the return, in 1829, of August Bournonville, after long years of training in Paris.
In the early years of the 19th Century, the international circulation of dance artists, already consolidated during the second half of the 18th Century, contributed to the popularization of new methods and the spread of new techniques, and furthered the continuous processes of assimilation and contamination. In Italy, the case of Salvatore Viganò, student of his father Onorato, but also a disciple of Dauberval, was one of the most significant. The same can be said of Carlo Blasis and Salvatore Taglioni, who, although in different measures, were both to carry their French education with them into Italy, at the same time also absorbing current Italian practices and methods. Another emblematic case is the education of August Bournonville, whose initial studies with Angiolini's student Vincenzo Galeotti merged with Bournonville's subsequent experiences at the school of the great Auguste Vestris.
Nevertheless, differences between France and Italy, in terms of taste, poetic and

dramatic lines, and production systems, as well – all of which had already characterized the second half of the 18th Century – remained less visible, but nonetheless profound in measure. This was due both to the influence of the artistic and cultural climate on the artists and to entrepreneurial logic. While the disciples of Gaspero Angiolini and Salvatore Viganò leaned toward a formula for ballet that had preponderant mimed sections and a minority presence of dance, in France, ballet tended to concede more and more space to academic dance, developing its technical vocabulary in a decisively expressive direction and sublimating in a poetic message the lightness, elegance and gracefulness sanctioned by the Académie Royale.

In early 19th-Century France, after the assertion of the "comedy" set in rural surroundings – so appreciated during the 1770s and -80s (notable in this regard are Maximilien Gardel and Dauberval during the reign of Louis XVI) – and after the Spanish-style ballets that were more or less faithful to the comedies by Beaumarchais, Oriental plots driven by the latest trends in literature and figurative arts began to appear. Similarly, Gothic and Renaissance revivalism also found new breathing space, as did the rediscovery of the fable, leading the creativity of the artists toward the discovery of Nordic legends and the mysterious myths of the Orient. Thus was the explosion of Romantic ballet attained, bringing with it the restlessness typical of literary, theatrical and musical production of analogous properties.

The ballet panorama of the 1830s and -40s was extremely varied, and that of the second half of the century no less so. The fantastical element that had been so dominant during the era of Romantic productions was to share public interest with adventurous tales and dances of a "national" character, for which new rhythms were also introduced: from the "Swiss" waltz, to the polka, mazurka and polonaise.

After the last ballets that would define a clean break with past (*Les Pages du Duc de Vendôme*, 1820; *Alfred le Grand*, 1822; *Cendrillon* [Cinderella], 1823; *La Sonnambule*, 1827; *La Belle au Bois Dormant* [The Sleeping Beauty], 1829), the great masterpieces of French Romantic ballet appeared in rapid succession: *La Sylphide* (1832), *Giselle* (1841), *La Péri* (1843) and *Catarina ou la Fille du Bandit* (1846, 1847).

In French Romantic ballet, the choreographic framework was that indicated by Noverre – a blending of pantomime and dance – even though the need to expand the communicative aspect of ballet would induce choreographers to try to exceed the structural limitations of French pantomime, appropriating some of the idioms from Italian mimic language to create a sort of "universal language".

In Italy, on the other hand, after the momentous period at La Scala when Salvatore Viganò (and Alessandro Sanquirico for the stage designs) would tower over the rest with productions of *Prometheus* (1812), *The Vestal* (1818) and *The Titans* (1819), the 1820s were to see the rise of names like Gaetano Gioia, Francesco Clerico and Giovanni Galzerani, to whom we owe titles that were to unequivocally differentiate stage production in Italy from that in France: *The Capture of Babylon* and *Marriage by Surprise* by Clerico (1821); *Gabriella di Vergy* and *Il Britanico* by Gioia (1822); and Galzerani's *Maria Stuarda* (Mary Stuart) and *Il Corsaro* (The Corsaire, 1826). In the Romantic era, on the other hand, we see a prudent compromise that allowed space for the newest trends in European taste. This explains the custom – common during the first half of the century – of inserting free-standing dance numbers in French academic style, giving to the dancers of "French rank" not a role within main adventure, but instead a space for their pure dance separate from the action.

In the musical sphere, the practice of collating extracts from well-known operas, current during the period saddling the turn of the 19th Century, was generally abandoned, and the figure of the ballet-music composer was institutionalized definitively, the role having previously been covered by either the orchestra conductors (like Florian Johann Deller and Johann Joseph Rodolphe, and Franz Aspelmayr for Noverre's works), the opera composers (Gluck, for example, for Angiolini's ballets) or by the choreographers themselves. This was a gradually conquered autonomy, which was justified by both the greater duration allotted to the ballet and the originality of its plots.

In contrast to how things had occurred in the 18th Century, when the choreographer had been urged to adhere to the dramaturgic text, in this period, the literary text sometimes represented only a pretext, as in the case of Charles Nodier's *Trilby, ou le lutin d'Argail* (Trilby, or the Goblin of Argail) for Filippo Taglioni's *La Sylphide,* in which themes of temptation and the prohibited dream gave life to a delightful love duet, enlivened by female craftiness and all the technical instruments available, to render the elusiveness of the fantastical character.

This was one of the aspects, together with plagiarism, that contributed – already in the 1700s – to the indispensability of the printed "Programme" for ballet performances. Despite this, choreographers who wished to defend against the problems of imitation and unearned attribution would have to wait until the institution of laws protecting authors' rights, that is, until the founding of the *Société des auteurs, compositeurs et editeurs de Musique* (1851) in France, and in Italy, of the equivalent *Società degli autori* (1882).

After the further maturation and evolution of dance, the 19th Century was to close with some splendid productions. From the wealth of French ballet transplanted to Russia, fascinating new titles emerged, like *The Sleeping Beauty*, a ballet that succeeded in harmonizing the aesthetic and technical qualities of both French and Italian traditions, in a composition that was perfectly balanced between emotion, moral content, political reference and "pleasure for the eyes". This ballet followed soon after the end-of-century Italian masterpiece, *Excelsior*. On a structural level, this "*gran ballo*", as it was called, although firmly anchored in the Italian trend toward Positivism and linked to the allegorical-celebratory tradition in ballet, displayed an openness to exchange with French dance, with which it shared a similar interest in pure dance and a more "modern" vision of choreographic composition.

These two ballets are of particularly significance as regards the process of liberating "*la danse proprement dite*", or pure dance, which, as Carlo Blasis had proposed, was indeed already being considered an autonomous artistic language.

The Foundation of Classical Ballet

Costume sketch attributed to Henri de Gissey of a dancer in a *ballet de cour*, ca. 1660, from the Victoria and Albert Museum, London. The costume expresses all the beauty and richness of the ballets organized at the French court during the reign of Louis XIV. The leather strips on the short skirt and the "Roman costume" breastplate are transformed into a glowing ensemble.

Louis XIV: the Sun King

Louis XIV played a decisive role in the birth of French academic dance and the establishment of its guidelines. His involvement served as a guarantee that dance would have a place in theatrical performances and insured the technical and stylistic quality of the ballets, through his establishment of a system of guidelines that was logical and in accordance with the aesthetic norms dictated by classical art.
He experimented directly with these norms himself in dances presented at court and in the *ballets de cour*, in which he took part, interpreting various roles.

This image portrays Louis XIV, not yet fifteen years of age, in the role of the god *Apollo* in *Ballet Royal de la Nuit*, the *ballet de cour* from 1653 that would earn him the title of "Sun King". The costume and its multicolored, feathered headdress are covered with resplendent golden rays, a manifest symbol of the interpretation of *Apollo* as being God of the Sun. This iconography was to be maintained throughout the 1700s, as is documented in the costume sketch by Louis-René Boquet for the ballet by Noverre, *Admète et Alceste*, reprinted on page 119.

Louis XIV is portrayed here in 1701, at the age of 63, by Hyacinthe Rigaud. The physical attitude and the positioning of his legs are clear marks of the elegant bearing and exquisite manners that made the Sun King famous in all the courts of Europe. A passionate admirer of dance, he participated directly in court performances until 1670, taking on various roles. In 1681, he then re-appeared in another god-like role (at the royal palace at Saint-Germain-en-Laye), that of Comus in *Le Triomphe de l'Amour*.

The Académie Royale de Danse

In 1661, at the explicit wish of Louis XIV, the Académie Royale de Danse, an association formed of *maîtres à danser* (dancing masters) from the families of the Parisian upper aristocracy, was founded. The institutional task of the Académie Royale was to establish the rules relative to dance technique and theory, with a formulation and terminology that would conform to those of the other academic disciplines (namely, fencing and riding).
The norms instituted by the Académie Royale were directed at all forms of dance, from that of the social ballrooms to theatrical dancing, but their primary function was the regulation of aristocratic dance in the grand balls given at court and in the *ballets de cour*. The adjusting of professional dance to courtly norms, as would also occur with new musical forms (the *tragédie lyrique* and *opéra-ballet*), was, in regard to the *ballet de cour*, essentially a consequence of the projection of social dancing onto a theatrical setting.
Consequently, if, in the *ballet de cour*, professional dancers adjusted their style to match that of the nobility (with whom they mixed during the course of a performance), in theatrical ballet, these same dancers also reproduced the techniques and style of aristocratic dancing, under the vigilant control of the Académie Royale, of which they were frequently members.
Returning to the codification of technical, stylistic and terminological principles, as established by the Académie Royale, the aristocracy was the first to be subjected to the new praxis. But, as the abbot Michel De Pure wrote in his *Idées des Spectacles anciens et nouveaux* (Paris, 1668), to dance at a courtly ball was more demanding for the nobility than was participation in a *ballet de cour*, because, while in the latter, the interpreters (whether *cavaliers* or *dames*), who were mixing with other dancing figures, felt "protected" by their masks and costumes, in the ballroom, they presented themselves to the critical view of other members of the court, who judged upon "*le bien et le mal dont l'Art et la Nature ont favorisé ou disgrasié*" ("the good and the bad which Art and Nature hath favored or disgraced") (pp. 117-118).
Such rules as those established by the Académie Royale, strict as they were, did not impose abstract motor schemes of pure invention, but rather a stylization of natural movement based on the principle of an idealized imitation of nature, as codified in classical art. The rhythms of the dances and the structure of the steps were gathered from the dances of certain French regions, from which they also took their names: the Minuet from Poitou and from Anjou, the Bourrée from Auvergne, the Passepied from Brittany, etc.
Posture was inspired by the structure of the body itself and by the natural movement of the arms while walking, as were the movement basics: *aplomb*, *en-dehors*, leg/arm opposition, the length of steps and the *effacements*. All these elements were highlighted in illustrated manuals, in which the similarities to both the codified models from other academic arts (above all, fencing) and the iconographic schemes from classical art are easily recognizable.

The Manuals

Dance manuals from the early 1700s are very precise in their analysis of the dynamics and rhythms of steps and the precise spatial trajectory of movements, and also in their descriptions of arm/leg coordination. Steps are dissected according to an extremely rational procedure, using a method of visualization that, as these illustrations attest, was, didactically speaking, very efficient.
In the images below from Pierre Rameau's 1725 text *Le Maître à danser*, which illustrate a *demi-coupé* (a basic dance step), the step appears dismembered into four parts, each one corresponding to one of the four phases of the step itself. The first figure corresponds to the starting position; the second shows the passing of the foot through 1st position; the third indicates the forward movement of the foot, with the legs still in *demi-plié;* and the fourth illustrates the completion of the transfer of weight and the body's rise *sur la pointe* (a term corresponding to today's *demi-pointe*). The numbers placed by the feet refer to explanations provided in the text.

The manuals contain not only rules for the correct execution of dances, but also, as can be read here on the frontispiece of the book by Pierre Rameau, instructions on proper society behavior.
In the figure to the right (the book's pre-frontispiece), we see the progression of a dance lesson. The *maître à danser* (dancing master) plays the violin himself, as he would have been expert in both disciplines (music and dance).
Among the notions imparted were also those of bowing and the removal of one's hat.

LE MAÎTRE
A DANSER.

QUI enſeigne la maniere de faire to
les differens pas de Danſe dans tou
la regularité de l'Art, & de condui
les Bras à chaque pas.

*Enrichi de Figures en Taille-douce, ſerva
de démonſtration pour tous les differe
mouvemens qu'il convient faire da
cet exercice.*

Ouvrage très-utile non-ſeulement à la Jeuneſſe
veut apprendre à bien danſer, mais encore aux p
ſonnes honnêtes & polies, & qui leur donne
regles pour bien marcher, ſaluer & faire les rever
ces convenables dans toutes ſortes de compagnies

Par le Sieur RAMEAU, *Maître à danſer des P
de Sa Majeſté Catholique la Reine d'Eſpagne.*

A PARIS,
Chez JEAN VILLETTE, ruë ſaint Jacq
à la Croix d'Or.

M. DCCXXV.
Avec Approbation, & Privilege du Roi.

In the images here to the right, from the same manual by Pierre Rameau, *Le Maître à danser*, one can recognize the difference between the basic bow for gentlemen (forward) and its equivalent for ladies. While keeping her feet close together, the Lady bends her knees only slightly, and out of propriety, she avoids lowering her gaze; the Gentleman bends his frame forward to look down, as a sign of deference, while advancing one leg.
Top: the basic bow.
Bottom: the passing bow, with the body "*effacé*" (see p. 30).
The difference between the figures from the pre-frontispiece (from the original 1725 edition) and these here to the right, illustrating the various bows (from the second English edition of 1731), points to the relatively high number of editions released, which is consistent with the remarkable diffusion of French dance in Europe.

In the images below, from same manual by Rameau, note the "obliged" phases that a nobleman was expected to respect during the removal of the hat preceding a bow.

Anatomical *and* Mechanical

LECTURES

UPON

DANCING.

WHEREIN

Rules and Institutions for that Art are laid down and demonſtrated.

As they were Read at the

Academy in *Chancery Lane.*

By JOHN WEAVER, Dancing Maſter.

Spartam quam nactus eſt, hanc ornat.

LONDON:

Printed for J. Brotherton, *and* W. Meadows, *at the* Black Bull *in* Cornhill; J. Graves, *near* White's *Chocolate Houſe in St.* James's *Street*; *and* W. Chetwood, *at* Cato's *Head in* Ruſſel *Street*, Covent Garden. M.DCC.XXI.

In reading the manuals, we also witness the extreme depth of the dancing masters' preparation and how its basis was rooted in anatomy.

Anatomical and Mechanical Lectures upon Dancing, published in London in 1721, is referred to as the first text of anatomy for use by dancers. It was authored by the English dancer and choreographer John Weaver, who, among his other writings, also penned essays of a historical nature about dance. Deeply cultured in a variety of areas, Weaver also had specific notions about anatomy, acquired from his studies of highly specialized texts, such as the two volumes of *De Motu Animalium*, published in 1685 by Giovanni Borelli.

Principles of Classical Ballet

The Aplomb

In the images from Pierre Rameau's manual, *Le Maître à danser* (Paris, 1725), one clearly perceives the aesthetic meaning of *aplomb* (derived from the Latin *plumbum*, or the metal lead), as a distinctive trait of courtly dancing.
By tradition, the vertical figure was a sign of cultural and social elevation, and it implied the natural and light ease in both gesture and movement that was so exalted in classical art.
In this same image, we see how, in terms of technique, the concept of *aplomb* would imply an erect body posture deriving from the alignment of the head, pelvis and feet in a perpendicular relationship to the floor, and how this alignment would be coordinated with an increase in the outward rotation of the feet to 90° in total (45° for each foot).

The **En-Dehors** *(Turn-Out)*

In academic dance, the *en-dehors* implied an outward rotation of the feet, increased to 45° for each foot (90° in total). This was fixed and equal for all, regardless of the individual body's ability to conform, its natural outward deviation being somewhere between 20-30° degrees.

In these images from Kellom Tomlinson's *The Art of Dancing Explained by Reading and Figures* (London, 1735), we can clearly grasp the principle objectives of the *en-dehors*: stability (as in fencing), aesthetics (the inner leg being aesthetically the most pleasing) and functionality as regards steps – i.e., a greater ability to cross the feet. The precision with which the natural outward rotation of the feet (20-30° from parallel) is reproduced in this large fresco of *Bacchus and Arianna* from Herculaneum in Italy (below, left) and in these two famous "ideal models" of ancient sculpture – the *Apollo del Belvedere* (center) and the *Medici Venus* (right) – testifies to the analytical observation of the human body in classical culture. The study of masterpieces of ancient art would constantly guide both the *maîtres à danser* (dancing masters) and the *maîtres de ballets* (choreographers) during the 17th and 18th Centuries.

These illustrations of fencing, taken from Diderot and d'Alembert's *Encyclopédie ou Dictionnaire raisonné des sciences des Arts et des Métiers* (1751-1772), clearly illustrate the 90° angle of the feet, created by the outward rotation of the hip joint (*en-dehors*), just as in dance. They also make explicit the functions of this – stability, readiness, and elegance in the movements of the legs and feet – and furthermore, they suggest how the two disciplines were in a state of reciprocity, as regards the education of young men from the upper classes.

The Arms

In the search for precision and stylistic accuracy, the arms were not to escape notice. Their dual function as regards balance – both technical and aesthetic – is comparable to that of a picture frame, in relation to the painting itself.
Rameau's manual *Le Maître à danser* devotes an entire chapter to the arms, elaborated with numerous illustrations in which he uses the method cited earlier of breaking down movement into its constituent parts and illustrating its trajectory visually, through which we can understand the importance given to theory, as an instrument of knowledge.

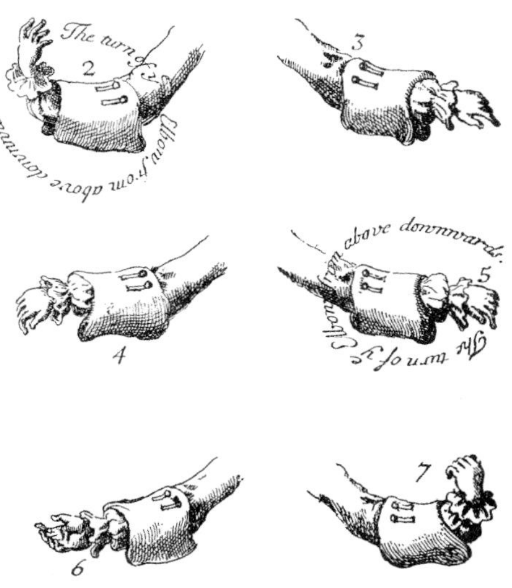

The perfect positioning and movements of the arms are illustrated through sketches and graphic instructions that show the complexity of the turning of the wrist (*rond du poignet*) and elbow (*rond du coude*). These rotations, technically very difficult to achieve, articulated the rhythm of a step, in accompaniment to the legs and movements of the rest of the body. The manual was re-issued in England in 1731, with new illustrations by George Bickham the Younger; thus, the captions here are written in English.

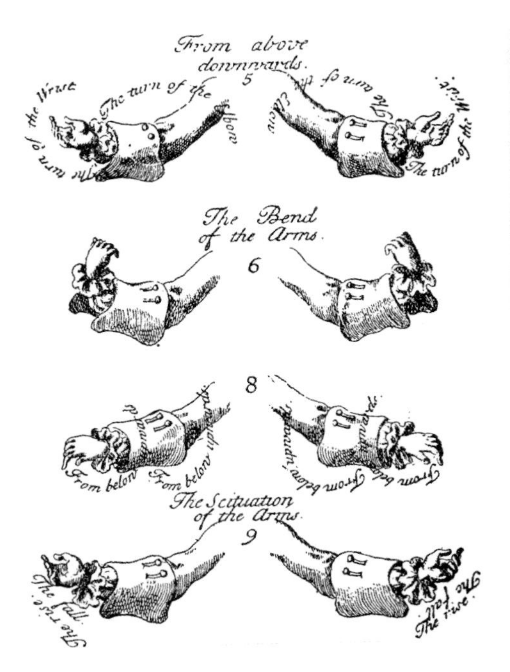

The Idealization of Gesture and Stylization of the Arms

Numerous images from various iconographic *repertoires* show the inspiration for the basic positioning of the head and arms as deriving from the rhetorical gestures of allegoric figures. This should not be surprising, as a large portion of the characters in the *ballets de cour* were indeed taken from the world of antiquity. Here below, left, the costume sketch by Jean Berain for *Le Triomphe de l'Amour* (1681) of the *Indian* from Bacchus' retinue highlights its own similarity to the allegories of *Conservatione* (above right) and *Abondanza* (Abundance; below), drawn by the Cavalier d'Arpino for the 1603 edition of Cesare Ripa's *Iconologia*. The arms take the same attitude, and the head is elegantly reclined in the direction of the raised hand, as if to accompany the gesture.

The Opposition of the Arms and Legs

As can be seen in the figure at the bottom left, in contrast to pictorial images – in which the attitude of the arms is typically related to the general posture or varies in accordance with the curve of the body – in the dancing figure, the rounded arm is always placed in opposition to the leg that is either forward or behind, in respect to the other; that is, it is understood to be an arm "in opposition".
This counter-positioning of leg and arm is inspired by the spontaneous swing of the arms in natural walking, as we see here in this 1772 *bas-relief* by L. C. Gori, entitled *La Danza delle Ore* (The Dance of the Hours), from the collection at the Palazzo Pitti in Florence. In advancing one foot, it is "natural" that the opposite arm also comes forward, creating a balance between the various parts of the body (upper/lower; right/left).

In the figure below, left, from Pierre Rameau's *Le Maître à danser* (1725), emphasis is given to the opposite arm by the raising of the hand, in a circular movement that begins low and finishes high. However, the inarticulate drawing (by Rameau himself) fails to highlight the slight drawing back of the shoulder corresponding to the arm extended to the side. This retraction spontaneously accompanies the opposition and, as such, is an integral element of the same.
The figure below, right, on the other hand, replicates the famous Paris Opera dancer Claude Ballon. As this is a portrait, rather than an illustration from a technical manual, the artist did not consider it necessary to respect the rules of opposition, and so, the raised arm corresponds instead to the leg that is forward.

Effacer l'Épaule ***(concealing the shoulder)***

The play of the shoulders, which is connected either to the crossing of the feet or to a couple's meeting, is a recurring theme, and it has various degrees of amplitude. Beginning with the retraction of one shoulder – an integral aspect of arm/leg opposition (see p. 29) – the angle at which the shoulders can be placed may be increased, depending on the expressive or rhythmic requirements. In this case, it is no longer a stylization of natural movement, but rather a gesture constructed according to the rules of "good taste". This gesture would come to be known as *effacer l'épaule* (concealing the shoulder by drawing it back), inasmuch as it refers to a movement of the shoulder in relation to the body and/or partner.
In the two images reprinted below, from Kellom Tomlinson's manual (1735), the dancers displace their shoulders (and bodies) onto the same diagonal, creating a "shoulder-to-shoulder" effect reminiscent of popular dances (see p. 71, right). One can also see how *effacer l'épaule* would have related exclusively to the shoulders and was not connected to the legs.

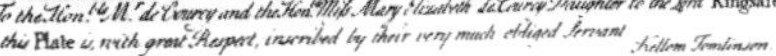

Also in this image with the foil, from Diderot and d'Alembert's *Encyclopédie*, we see that *effacer l'épaule* is an expression that regards only the shoulders, even if its principle function is to hide the body from the attack of the rival's sword. This example demonstrates how terminology was shared by fencing and dance alike, although the objectives in actual usage were not the same.

Dance and Ballet in Lyric Opera and *Opéra-Ballet* during the Late 1600s

These pages, taken from the *Dictionnaire des théâtres de Paris*, by Claude and François Parfaict (1767), which relate to the opera *Thesée* (Theseus) by Jean-Baptiste Lully and Philippe Quinault (Paris Opera, 1675), demonstrate the presence of ballet in each section of the opera: six times in total, from the Prologue through all five acts (closing each scene).
The performers (right page), although considered an integral element of the action (*Acteurs du Ballet*, or Actors of the Ballet), portrayed generic figures (Greeks, Old People, Spirits, Inhabitants of the Enchanted Island), as the principal roles (Medea, Theseus, Minerva, etc.) were assigned to the singers.

TH 409

des Œuvres de l'Auteur. Cette Tragédie a reparu au Théatre. *Histoire du Th. Franç. année* 1700.

THÉSÉE, Tragédie lyrique en cinq actes, avec un Prologue, de M. *Quinault*, Musique de M. *Lully*, représentée par l'Académie Royale de Musique, à S. Germain en Laye, devant le Roi le Vendredi 11 Janvier 1675. & ensuite à Paris au mois d'Avril, in-4°. Paris, & tome I. du Recueil général des Opéra, *Extrait*, *Mercure de France*, *Décembre* 1729. 2e *volume*, p. 3099-3112.

ACTEURS DU PROLOGUE.

Deux Graces. Mlles Bony & Piesche.
Deux Amours. Les Sieurs Marotte & Lanneau.
Bacchus. Le Sieur La Grille.
Vénus. Mlle Beaucreux.
Cérès. Mlle La Borde.
Mars. Le Sieur Godonesche.
Bellonne. Le Sieur Dauphin.

BALLET.

Suivans de Cérès.
Les Sieurs Noblet, Barazé, Lestang & Blondy.
Suivantes de Cérès.
Les Sieurs Bonnard, Boutteville, Arnal & de Berne.
Suivans de Bacchus. Le Sieur Dolivet pere.
Les Sieurs Chicanneau, Le Chantre & Pesant.
Suivantes de Bacchus.
Les Sieurs Mayeu, Bernier, Charlot & Dolivet *fils*.

ACTEURS DE LA TRAGÉDIE.

Æglé. Mlle Aubry.
Cléone, Confidente d'Æglé. Mlle Brigogne.
Arcas, Confident d'Egée. Le Sieur Morel.
La Grande Prêtresse de Minerve. Mlle Verdier.
Egée. Le Sieur Gaye.

Tome V S

410 TH

Médée. Mlle Saint Christophe.
Dorine, Confidente de Médée. Mlle Beaucreux.
Thésée. Le Sieur Clediere.
Minerve. Mlle Des Fronteaux.
Vieillards. Les Sieurs Tholet & Miracle.
La Rage. Le Sieur Jollain.
Le Désespoir. Le Sieur Le Febvre.
Bergéres. Mlles Desfronteaux, Bony, Verdier & Piesche.
Habitant de l'Isle enchantée. Le Sieur La Grille.

ACTEURS DU BALLET.

ACTE I. *Sacrificateurs.* Le Sieur Beauchamps.
Les Sieurs Desmatins, Favre, Pesant, Favier C. Blondy, Joubert & Foignart C.
Prêtresses dansantes.
Les Sieurs Magny, Favier L. Noblet, Germain, Pecourt & Bouteville.

ACTE II. *Grecs.*
Les Sieurs Mayeu, Barazé, Dolivet *fils* & Charlot.
Grecques.
Les Sieurs Joubert, Arnal, Lestang & Boutteville.
Vieillards.
Les Sieurs Dolivet & Le Chantre.
Vieilles.
Les Sieurs Bonnard & Magny.

ACTE III. *Lutins.* Le Sieur Beauchamps.
Les Sieurs Favier L. Favier C. Lestang, Favre, Magny, Joubert, Foignart, Chicanneau, Desairs, De Benne & Pecourt..
Un fantome. Le Sieur Alard.

ACTE IV. *Habitans de l'Isle enchantée.*
Les Sieurs Magny, Pecourt, Foignart, Lestang, La Pierre & Favier L.
Habitantes de l'Isle enchantée.
Les Sieurs Noblet, Chicanneau, Favier C. Royer, Boutteville & Germain.

ACTE V. *Un Grand Seigneur de la Cour d'Egée.*
Le Sieur Beauchamps.
Courtisans,
Les Sieurs Favier L. Lestang, Favre & Magny.

Opéra-ballet, commonly referred to simply as *ballet,* is the form of lyric choreography born at the end of the 17th Century, and it consisted of a succession of scenes or acts (from three to five), in which the contents were formed around brief little tales or comedies. These were enclosed within the single acts and connected together by a generic "red thread".
In *L'Europe galante* (1697), for example, outlined here in the same *Dictionnaire,* all four of the ballet's *entrées* are in praise of love, showing the different ways of loving in four European countries: France, Spain, Italy and Turkey. It was performed by turn-of-the-century stars at the Paris Opera: Michel Blondy, Claude Ballon and Marie-Thérèse Subligny.

462 EU

Italien en cinq actes, ſuivi d'un divertiſſement, repréſenté pour la premiére fois le Samedi 19 Mai 1745. *Sans Extrait.*

EUGÉNE, *ou la* RENCONTRE, Comédie en cinq actes & en vers de huit ſyllabes, par Etienne *Jodelle*, repréſentée devant le Roi Henri II. après la Tragédie de *Cléopatre*, à l'Hôtel de Rheims à Paris, en 1552. imp. dans les Œuvres de cet Auteur. *Hiſt. du Th. Fr. année* 1552.

EUNUQUE, (l') Comédie en cinq actes & en vers de M. de la *Fontaine*, 1654. imp. la même année, Paris, Courbé, in-4°. *Hiſt. du Th. Fr. année* 1654.

EUROPE, Comédie héroïque en cinq actes & en vers, de M. *Deſmareſts*, imp. Paris, Le Gras, 1643. in-4°. & in-12. *Hiſt. du Th. Fr. année* 1643.

EUROPE (l') GALANTE, Ballet en cinq Entrées, dont la premiére forme le Prologue, par M. de la *Motte*, Muſique de M. *Campra*, repréſenté par l'Académie Royale de Muſique, le Jeudi 24 Octobre 1697. in-4°. Ballard, & tome VI. du Recueil général des Opéra.

ACTEURS. I. ENTRÉE.

Vénus. Mlle Clément.
La Diſcorde. Le Sieur Deſvoyes.

BALLET.

Graces. Mlles Dufort, Clément & Freville.

II. ENTRE'E. *La France.*

Silvandre. Le Sieur Thévenard.
Philene. Le Sieur Boutelou.
Céphiſe. Mlle Deſmatins.

EU 463

BALLET.

Un Berger. Le Sieur Blondy.

III. ENTRE'E. *L'Eſpagne.*

D. Pedro. Le Sieur Chopelet.
D. Carlos. Le Sieur Hardouin.

BALLET.

Eſpagnol, Eſpagnolette. Le Sieur Balon & Mlle Dufort.

IV. ENTRE'E. *L'Italie.*

Octavio. Le Sieur Du Meſny.
Olympia. Mlle Moreau.

BALLET.

More & Moreſſe. Le Sieur Balon & Mlle Subligny.

V. ENTRE'E. *La Turquie.*

Zaïde. Mlle Deſmatins.
Roxane. Mlle Rochois.
Zuliman. Le Sieur Thevenard.

BALLET.

Sultanes. Mlles Subligny, Carré, Dufort, Freville, Le Maire & Ruelle.

IIe REPRISE du Ballet de l'*Europe galante*, le Mardi 18 Mai 1706. 2e édit. in-4°. Ballard.

ACTEURS. I. ENTRÉE.

Vénus. Mlle Pouſſin.
La Diſcorde. Le Sieur Mantienne.

BALLET.

Les Graces. Mlles Prevoſt, Guyot & Subligny.

II. ENTRE'E. *La France.*

Silvandre. Le Sieur Thévenard.
Philene. Le Sieur Boutelou.
Céphiſe. Mlle Pouſſin.
Doris. Mlle Dupeyré.

BALLET.

Un Berger. Le Sieur Blondy.

V iv

These images from the same 1767 *Dictionnaire des théâtres de Paris* by the Parfaict Brothers reproduce the facts and structure of the first performance of Rameau's *opéra-ballet* entitled *Les Indes galantes* (Paris Opera, 1735), which, like *L'Europe galante*, was classified simply as *ballet*.
It is evident that the danced sections (also called *ballet*) would have been present in every act (*entrées*), beginning with the Prologue; and it is similarly clear that the dancers were generic characters and would not have had any roles within the main plot, inasmuch as they were there to accompany the singers, with dances that were matched to the place and event. Prime examples would be the *Peruvian* from the first staging (below, left page) and the *Savages*, from the reprise on March 10, 1736 (below, right page).

158 IN

1654. in 12. *Hist. du Th. Franç. année* 1654.

C'est le même sujet d'*Hermenigilde*, de M. de la *Caprenede*.

INDES (les) GALANTES, Ballet héroïque en trois actes avec un Prologue de M. *Fuselier*, Musique de M. *Rameau*, représenté par l'Académie Royale de Musique, le Mardi 23 Août 1735. in 4°. Paris, Ballard, & Tome XV. du Recueil général des Opéra. *Extrait*, *Mercure de France*, *Août* 1735. *pag*. 2035-2046. Réflexions sur cet Opéra, *idem*, Novembre 1735. p. 2367 2372.

ACTEURS DU PROLOGUE.

Hébé. Mlle Eremans.
Bellone. Le Sieur Cuignier.
L'Amour. Mlle Petitpas.

BALLET.

Le Sieur Dupré & Mlle Rabon.
Un Plaisir. Mlle Le Breton.

ACTE I. *Le Turc Généreux.*

Osman, Bacha. Le Sieur Dun.
Emilie, Esclave d'Osman. Mlle Péllissier.
Valere, amant d'Emilie. Le Sieur Jélyotte.

BALLET.

Matelots.

Le Sieur Maltaire 3. & Mlle Mariette.

II. ENTRE'E. *Les Incas du Pérou.*

Huascar, Inca. Le Sieur Chassé.
Phani-Palla. Mlle Antier.
D. Carlos. Le Sieur Jélyotte.

BALLET.

Un Péruvien. Le Sieur D. Dumoulin.
Une Péruvienne. Mlle Le Breton.

IN 159

III. ENTRÉE. *Les Fleurs*, Fête Persane.

Tacmas, Prince Persan. Le Sieur Tribou.
Aly. Le Sieur Person.
Zaire, Princesse Circassienne. Mlle Eremans.
Fatime, Princesse Georgienne, déguisée en Esclave Polonois. Mlle Petitpas.

BALLET.

Bostangi. Le Sieur Dupré.
Zéphyre. Le Sieur D. Dumoulin.
La Rose. Mlle Sallé.
Borée. Le Sieur Javillier L.

L'Académie Royale de Musique reprit ce Ballet le Samedi 10 Mars 1736. avec une nouvelle Entrée intitulée *Les Sauvages*, paroles & Musique des mêmes Auteurs, 2e édition du Ballet des *Indes Galantes*, avec le nouvel acte in 4°. Paris, Ballard, 1736. Extrait de l'Entrée des *Sauvages*. *Mercure de France*, *Mars*, 1736. p. 534 536.

PROLOGUE.

Comme ci-dessus, 23 *Août* 1735.

Ire ENTRÉE. *Les Incas du Pérou.*

Idem, que le 23 *Août.*

IIe ENTRÉE. *Le Turc généreux.*

Idem, que le 23 *Août.*

III. ENTRE'E. *Les Fleurs*, Fête Persane retouchée.

Tacmas. Le Sieur Tribou.
Fatime. Mlle Petitpas.
Atalide. Mlle Eremans.
Roxane. Mlle Bourbonnois.

BALLET.

Zéphyre. Le Sieur D. Dumoulin.
La Rose. Mlle Sallé.
Borée. Le Sieur Javillier L.

160 IN

IV. ENTRE'E. *Les Sauvages*, nouvel acte.

Damon. Le Sieur Jélyotte.
D. Alvar. Le Sieur Dun.
Zima. Mlle Pelissier.
Adario. Le Sieur Cuvillier.

BALLET.

Sauvages. Le Sieur Dupré.
Le Sieur Maltaire 3. & Mlle Mariette.
Amazones Françoises. Mlles Carville, Rabon, & Du Rocher.

IIIe REPRISE du Ballet des *Indes Galantes*, le Jeudi 27 Décembre 1736. pour être joué alternativement avec l'Opéra de *Médée & Jason*.

IVe REPRISE du Ballet des *Indes Galantes*, le Mardi 28 Mai 1743. 3e édition in-4°. Paris, Ballard.

ACTEURS DU PROLOGUE.

Hébé. Mlle Fel.
Bellone. Le Sieur Albert.

BALLET.

Le Sieur Dupré & Mlle Rabon.
Un Plaisir. Mlle Le Breton.

I. ENTRE'E. *Le Turc généreux.*

Osman. Le Sieur Le Page.
Emilie. Mlle Le Maure.
Valere. Le Sieur Jélyote.
Une Matelotte. Mlle Fel.

BALLET.

Esclave Afriquain. Le Sieur Lany.
Une Matelotte. Mlle Camargo.

II. ENTRE'E. *Les Incas du Pérou.*

Huascar, Inca. Le Sieur Chassé.
Phani Palla. Mlle Chevalier.
D. Carlos. Le Sieur Jélyotte.

BALLET.

Un Inca. Le Sieur Ghérardi.

The Performance Space

Of all the activities that occupied the court, dancing was, as we have seen, one of the most demanding, as well as one of the most socially significant. It was a form of entertainment reserved for members of the aristocracy, of which one part (the lower ranks) formed the spectators and the other (the nobility closest to the sovereign) actively participated, executing dances in couples in the presence of onlookers and the king.
Court dancing was organized according to quite rigid protocol, which called for two opening group dances, followed by dances executed by single pairs, the order of which also followed hierarchical rules.
In this engraving from the 1725 manual *Le Maître à danser* by Pierre Rameau (Dancing Master of the Pages of Her Majesty, the Queen of Spain), the royal throne is seen clearly in a position slightly higher than the level on which the dances took place. The area reserved for dancing was delineated in rectangular form and reduced in dimensions proportional to the extremely contained spatial development of the choreography.

It also appears evident that the elaborate choreographic designs and numerous movements of the body *en tournant* (turning) were not conceived to be observed from above; ladies and gentlemen alike used turns and *effacements* (changes in angulation of the torso achieved through the drawing back of one shoulder [*épaule*]) to create a complex play of shoulders and glances, in which they could unfurl all their bravura: from gracious carriage and technically precise execution, to the musicality of both steps and gesture.

Although from twenty years later, this extremely particularized 1745 depiction by Charles Nicolas Cochin le Jeune of the celebration organized at Versailles on the occasion of the wedding between the Dauphin of France and the Infanta of Spain demonstrates the continuity of praxis in court dancing between the respective reigns of Louis XIV and Louis XV.
The space reserved for dancing is rectangular, inscribed at the salon's perimeter and surrounded by the entire court, which is arranged on various levels, according to hierarchy. Nevertheless, as in the preceding engraving, it is the position of the sovereign that establishes the location of the most privileged viewpoint and, consequently, the orientation of the dance.
From their postures and arm positions (the lady is holding up her dress), it appears that the lady and gentleman are performing the Minuet, the only dance that does not require the complex wrist and arm movement described earlier on page 27.

In this theatrical performance at the royal court of Versailles during the 1674 feast *Les Divertissements de Versailles*, notice the arrangement of the king and court during a theater performance – in this case, Molière's *The Imaginary Invalid*.
Here, we are no longer looking at a performance in which the members of the court are both spectators and performers; and the area reserved for the performance is totally separated from the public.
The arrangement of the public in relation to the king is clearly established with respect to hierarchical order, with the visual enjoyment of the performance depending more or less on one's position in this order. But in its entirety, the general spatial organization reproduces, in reduced scale, the same configuration and relationships between the performing space and the spectator as in a public theater. The king is placed front and center, establishing his favored and privileged viewpoint.

These two photographs show the theater at the longtime residence in Ludwigsburg (near Stuttgart) of the Dukes of Württemberg. Although restored in the early 19th Century, the theater preserves its original mid-18th-Century structure.
The royal box is located at the furthest point directly opposite to the stage and is slightly raised in respect to it. The privileged viewpoint is, therefore, frontal and slightly higher than the level of the stage, which, at the same time, is strongly inclined toward the orchestra (raked). The wings are painted, and the dimensions gradually reduce as one proceeds upstage, creating the illusion of distance.

Male and Female Roles in Pair Dancing

In common with court dancing, the movements that appeared in ballets presented within an opera or *opéra-ballet* were stylistic re-workings of dances originating in certain regions of France, filtered by the choreographers and adjusted to the guidelines of the Académie Royale.
All these dances maintained a strict geometric structure. This was based on specular principles, just as in the applied arts and in the new configuration of the French garden, introduced at royal residences under Louis XIV.
This type of structure, being symmetrical, was defined as "regular", distinguishing it from an "irregular" structure, in which the path taken by the dancers, moving parallel to each other, would create an asymmetrical pattern.
In mixed pair dancing, the geometry and, above all, the specular mirroring of choreographic movements made it difficult to differentiate between male and female roles, which is why the "dialogue" between the performers came to be simulated through delightful shoulder games (see p. 30, upper figures), using the formula *vis-à-vis, dos-à-dos* and shoulder-to-shoulder, and with movements *en tournant* (circular) that rendered the dance as meticulous as it was refined and delicate.

This photograph of the gardens at the residence Het Loo in the Dutch city of Apeldoorn, designed by Daniel Marot in the French style (1686-1702), shows a "regular" division of the various spaces and elements, inspired by rational and rigorous criteria. Note the specular placement of the green squares on either side of the central axis of the garden's symmetry.

Regular and Irregular Figures

In the two figures below – from *Recueil de danses* by R. A. Feuillet (1704) and Tomlinson's 1735 *The Art of Dancing*, respectively – we see how the symmetrical/specular composition, perfectly recognizable in the trajectory of the dancers (left), would have corresponded to a vertical vision of the body (right).

The two letters "q" and "p" – set next to each other in the figure below, left – express visually the specular principle, as explained in the manuals, while the double "p" in the figure on the right indicates the parallel path followed by a lady and gentleman. In the specular, or "regular", path on the left, the two dancers execute paths that are counter-positioned. In the image on the right, from Pierre Rameau's *Abbrégé de la nouvelle méthode dans l'art d'écrire ou de traçer toutes sortes de danses de ville*, the dancers move in harmony (as if linked) on a parallel path, thus drawing an "irregular" figure.

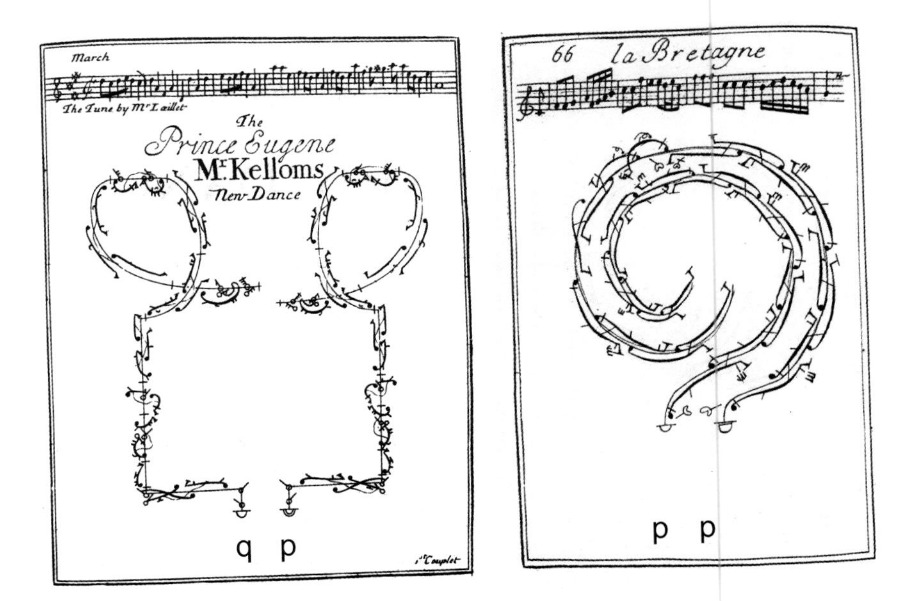

Characters and Symbols in the *Ballet du Cour*

The following images are presented with the aim of comparing diverse character types. While some of these do not relate to specific ballets, others concern the costumes designed by Henri de Gissey for Ballet Royal de la Nuit (1653), or Jean Berain's costume sketches for *Le Triomphe de l'Amour* (1681), created by Lully, in collaboration with Pierre Beauchamps.
At first glance, a substantial difference is evident between the figures with sumptuous garments and in noble poses, and the others that, although positioned in equally dignified attitudes, are distinguished by clothing that is also elegant, but more informal. These characters are, in turn, differentiated by their positions and costumes from the allegories and fantasy figures, for which the artist resorts to the bizarreness of Baroque theater, simultaneously making use of symbolism from classical art.
The costumes used for *héroïques* characters (below, right) conform to current female clothing: the garments are heavy, even droopy; the fabrics are richly decorated; and the puffed sleeves are wide and light.
The costumes for high-ranking male characters (below, left) are equally sumptuous, as regards both structure and fabrics, which are thickly encrusted with precious embroidery. The structure combining a tight-fitting bodice with a short tunic was inspired by the military dress of ancient Rome (thus, they were labeled "Roman costumes"). The man's costume is nevertheless also embellished with wide, rounded cuffs made of light material, which emerge from the tight-fitting sleeves.
Both characters have a courtly carriage: composed, and positioned in conventional gestures garnered from classical iconography. With one arm slightly raised and rounded, and often carrying a symbol of divinity (Neptune with his trident, for example), the other arm is counter-positioned low and open to the side, with the hand emphatically outstretched. The head is elegantly reclined to the side of the rounded arm, in a noble pose that would come to be known in the 18th Century as *abandon*.

Stylistically similar to the courtly figures, the characters that we see here form the "gentlemen's parade"designed by Jean Berain (1681): the *Indian* (from Bacchus' retinue) and the *Nymph* (from Orithyia's), among others. The positioning in these figures is equally "noble", and the clothing is lavish. The fundamental difference from the *noble* character is in the shorter garment, which seems to imply a dance that is elegant, yet dynamic (within the limits of academic norms). In fact, the fluttering of the *Nymph's* costume, as well as that of the costume worn by the *Bacchante* (bottom), is indicative of dynamism and agility.

The "trades" from the *Ballet de la Nuit* (1635) present a distinct contrast – in an accentuated, realistic way – which is revealed as much by their costumes as by their gestures.
The costumes for certain allegories are decidedly "deformed", while in others, the predominant characteristic could be said to be a well-studied oddity, produced by the bundling together on their bodies of specific symbols or peculiarities that recall the instruments of their respective professions. Here, below: the allegories of *Ignis Fatuus* (Fatuous Fire), the *Night Hour*, the *Goldsmith* and the *Architect*.

This *Triton's* body is covered with fish scales and seaweed. His tunic is fringed in the guise of seaweed, and the corals and marine plants on his head form a rich, multicolored headpiece. The character is shown blowing into a horn made of shell, as prescribed in classical iconographic tradition (the sound would have calmed storms and announced the arrival of Neptune). These symbols were to remain in ballet through the 18th Century, adapting to the new fashions in costuming (see pp. 50 and 118).

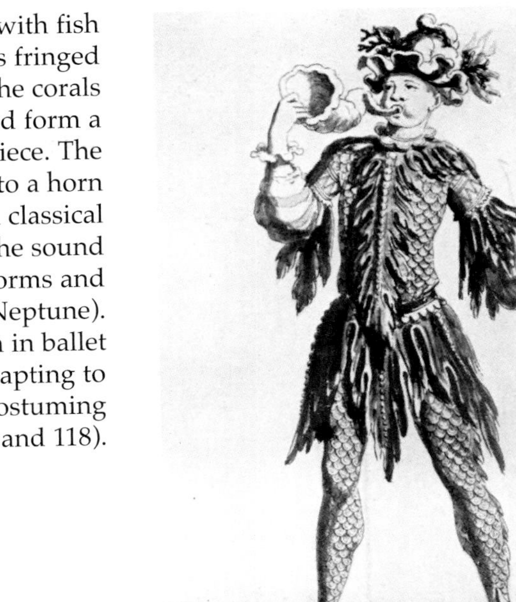

The costume for *River* also imitates the schemes from iconographic traditions: the cape recalls the flow of water, the decorations are re-workings of water-plant themes, and the symbol he holds is an oar, embellished as a scepter. The pose is matched to the costume's general structure (which conforms to the Roman style), and the oar as scepter underscores the character's regal nature.

These images point to a standardization of expressions, determined by the presence of masks that completely covered the dancers' faces. The features of this *Rustico* (a rustic character), highly accentuated as in Greek art, indicate the generic nature of the movements performed by these characters and their integration into conventional typology.
The molds on the right – conserved, together with the masks, at the Musée de l'Opéra de Paris – demonstrate the custom of producing numerous images of the same type.

The two images below, also from the Musée de l'Opéra in Paris, show front and profile views of a dancer wearing a classical mask, which completely covers his face, with the exception of the openings for the eyes and mouth.

The Role of Scenery

In all of the performances presented either at the courts or in public theaters, scenery (*la décoration*) fulfilled a central role in how the action was conducted and indeed in the success of the entire performance. Complex machinery designed by artists such as Giacomo Torelli and operated by skilled technicians had the function of raising or lowering platforms that were disguised as wagons or clouds. These platforms were sturdy and strong enough to carry more than one person, and the cables were also sufficiently robust to allow for the transport of both people and objects. Through the dense clouds (called *gloires*, or glories), divinities would appear "*ex machina*"; Pluto and Persephone might emerge from under the stage, sitting on their luxurious thrones; carriages driven by monsters came to skirt Medea away into the sky above Creon's burning palace. This practice, common in theaters all across Europe and in all types of performances – from lyric opera to ballet, from English pantomime to the Théâtre Italien in Paris – was maintained throughout the 1700s. And it was still recognizable in ballets of the 1800s: in the flight of the *Zephyrs* in *Flore et Zéphyr* by Charles-Louis Didelot (1796) and in the Romantic *Sylphides*.

This engraving of a drawing by Jean Berain, reproduced to the left, shows the scenery for Jean-Baptiste Lully's opera *Isis* – the final scene of Act V.
The divinities are descending from the heavens to receive *Isis*.

The drawing by Jean Berain reproduced below relates to the scenery for Lully's opera *Phaéton* (1683; final scene of Act V).
The impudent *Phaéton* is struck down with lightning by *Jupiter*, as punishment for having taken the carriage that crosses the sky daily to bring light to the earth, which belongs to his father, the sun-god *Helios*.

Ballet, Fashion and Tradition in the 18th Century

Antoine Watteau, *Venetian Pleasures*, 1718; National Gallery of Scotland, Edinburgh. Note the presence of the *panier* (crinoline), which increases the lateral dimensions of the skirt.

Changing Tastes

Les Éléments, the *opéra-ballet* performed at the Paris Opera in 1725, has generally been considered as an attempt to revive the traditions of 17th-Century *ballet de cour*. It had, in fact, first been performed for the royal courts in 1721, at the Parisian Tuileries palace, where it was danced by none other than Louis XV, who was yet to celebrate his twelfth birthday. A sampling still exists of the costume sketches for this ballet, designed by Claude Gillot, successor to Jean Berain the Younger, and engraved by Gillot's student Joullain.

The figures reproduced on the following pages, in addition to exposing the highly personal style of the artist, point above all to the profound changes in French style between the end of Louis XIV's reign and the regency of Philippe of Orleans (1715-1722). The figures are all dressed in costumes constructed in such a way as to mirror the new fashions in contemporary clothing (see painting below).

Nevertheless, it can also be observed in these same images that, not only was the costuming for ballet undergoing a renewal, but also, there was also a certain stylistic homogenization, in which the differences between "noble" characters and "fantastic" ones, between "courtesans" and allegories, were becoming visibly blurred.

Jean-Baptiste Pater, *The Picnic,* ca. 1720; Nelson-Atkins Museum of Art, Kansas City, Missouri

We now stand at the threshold of an ulterior transformation in the stage costume, which, like women's clothing, has not undergone structural modification for many years, despite an increase in both luxury and girth (even to the point of excess) (see p. 122). This process will find its equivalent in the academic ballets, in which exhibition itself becomes the objective and is transformed into a contest of virtuosity between dancers.

As regards style, the influence of Rococo on dance during the period saddling the mid-18th Century was so profound as to bestow upon ballet the role of amplifying and magnifying the trends in Rococo fashion, all for the pleasure of a public eager for curiosities and virtuosic effects.

The two images here (below) compare the costume of a *Triton* (right) with the *Habit de Roy* worn by Louis XV in 1721 (left). The construction of the two costumes is practically identical, and the strong resemblance in foot- and headwear infers a standardization in men's costumes. In both cases, the bodice, with its tight fit and shoulder decorations, is extended into a puffed *tonnelet* (a transformation of the earlier Roman tunic), that is, a wide, short skirt that is similar in length to a fashionable redingote and subdivided into sections, with a trimming near the lower hem. Structurally comparable, the costumes are distinguishable by their decorations, which emphatically accentuate the distinctive aspects of each character. The most highly characterized elements on the *Triton*'s costume are the unicorn horn and surrounding foliage on the head and the fish scales that cover the bodice. The costume worn by the *King*, on the other hand, is distinguished by its luxurious cape and elaborate headdress in the form of a turban, with a crown brimming with feathers, intended as a mark of nobility.

The figure below, left, and the figure on the previous page, right, compare a *Naiad* and a *Triton*, female and male versions of the fantastical aquatic character generally employed in the cortege of the god Neptune. In addition to the similar poses, we can see how the rotundity of the male *tonnelet* seems reproduced, although in reduced dimensions, in the female's garment, almost as if to create a sort of symmetry.
The garment worn by the *Naiad* (below, left), on the other hand, recalls the fashions of the times, the character's manifestation being signaled by the ornamentation on the costume: scales on the garment and showy corals on the head, accompanied by aquatic plants, and then a trimming of tri-lobated shells on the garment's edge.
Turning our attention to the *Faun* (below, right): despite the monstrous goat-like mask and striking headdress of forest leafage, which tend to confer an accentuated *grotesque* aspect upon the character – as does his chest being only half-covered by a panther skin thrown over one shoulder – he also sports an elegant and conventional *tonnelet* decorated with flowers, which, together with the gallant placement of the hand on his hip, restores to the character the necessary gentlemanliness of the epoch.
Also notable is the asymmetrical placement of the feral fur, which crosses his chest obliquely, leaving it half-uncovered. This diagonal cut is an unequivocal sign of Rococo's predilection for oblique lines, and it will be found in *Faun* costumes throughout the 1700s, as well as in costumes for Noverre ballets by Louis-René Boquet, after the former's neoclassical re-visitation of this theme (see p. 103).

These additional images relating to the costumes designed by Gillot for the *opéra-ballet Les Éléments* (1721) place in relief how the costumes for different female characters could be of identical construction: in this case, the two versions of the *Hours* (night and day) and the *Gardener*.
The allegory of the *Hours* (a fantastical character; two figures above) is distinguishable from the *Gardener* (a realistic character; below) only by the iconographic evocations inserted into the costume. Bat wings, a nocturnal variant of the butterfly wings that are also used in various versions of the *Day Hour* by Gillot, characterize the *Night Hour*; both *Hours* carry crowns of medals, with the hours written in Roman numerals, articulating the sections of the garment in exactly the same manner as the shells do in the costume worn by the *Naiad*.

Rather noticeable among these characters is the quite original version of *Folly*, in which the stylish *panier "à la mode"* supports a series of concentric frills, creating an impression of vibration that recalls the instability and fickleness of folly.
This is not a re-working of the traditional costume scheme for a female version of *Fou* (Madman), but is instead a rather original variation. In the same album of engravings, female and male costumes for the allegory *Folly* appear with the more typical markings: triangle-shaped fabric (in the garments and headwear) with small bells attached and a *marotte* (jester's stick).

These two early 18th-Century *Faun* masks, from the collection at the Musée de l'Opéra de Paris, present the accentuated, grotesque traits traditionally attributed to this role in ballet and also display the standardization of "in character" roles. Next to the leather mask is the mold from which the model was reproduced.

Aesthetics Dominant during the 1730s and -40s

On the following pages, several costumes by Jean-Baptiste Martin, dating back to the early 1730s, will be analyzed. These bear witness to the trends dominant in costumes of this period for both men and women, and they demonstrate how ballet costumes were subjected to a structural codification that would be preserved for more than thirty years.

Female garments have by now assumed the characteristic ovoid shape that widens out over the hips, due to the presence of a *panier* (crinoline), which consists of a support made of cane rods or whale bones, held together by ribbons and strings. The lateral dimensions of the male *tonnelet* have also increased, in proportion to female garment; and it has become more rigid, further developing the shape of a *tonneau* (barrel), from which the name *tonnelet* (little barrel) derives.

Noteworthy in Martin's drawings are the poses, which seem perfectly consistent with the costumes and are characterized by expressive nuances and technical refinements. The similarity of such poses to those used by Louis-René Boquet in his costume sketches for ballets by Noverre confirms the reliability of these poses from a technical and expressive viewpoint, offering at the same time elements that are useful in identifying the "genre" of the character's dancing style. The indications referred to here may be vague and conventional, but they are nonetheless useful in gathering the differences and similarities within the system of genres codified in academic ballet (*sérieux-héroique, demi-caractère* and *comique*).

The *panier*, so named due to its similarity to a basket, was the supporting structure in women's dresses, as we see diagrammed in the sketch below and documented in the painting by Watteau on p. 48.

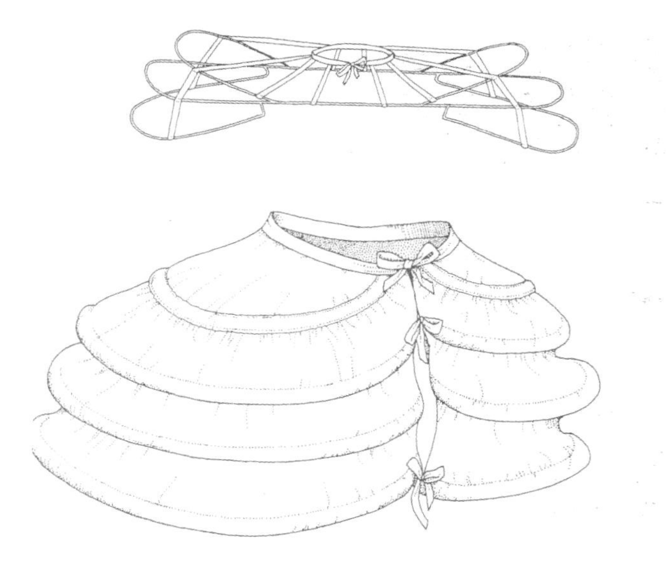

Differences and Analogies between Genres

The costumes of the *Faun* and *Dryad* (lower figure) are practically identical to those of the *Follower of Flora* and *Follower of Zephyr* (upper figure). Both male dancers wear luxurious feather-adorned headdresses, and the fabrics are, on the whole, precious and richly inlaid. The only substantial difference is one of ornamentation. The costumes of the *Follower of Flora* and *Follower of Zephyr* are interwoven with flowers and garlands that form a geometric motif similar to a floral festoon. The *Faun* and *Dryad*, on the other hand, each have a sort of surcoat that simulates wild furs. This partially covers the costume, cutting obliquely across in a manner reminiscent of the *Faun* costume by Gillot (see p. 51), although their surcoats differ from Gillot's in terms of the conventional function of symbolic evocation.
The same balance of similarities and differences can be noted in their gestures. In both couples, the legs and arms are positioned in an elegant and technically accurate manner. Nevertheless, certain differences – as subtle and formal as those of the costumes themselves – deserve consideration.

The extremely linear positions (of the arms and legs) in the *Follower of Zephyr* and *Follower of Flora*, the clarity of the figure's design and the grand dignity in the manners all contribute to give the impression of a *sérieux* genre. The "looser" position of the other couple – the *Faun* and *Dryad* – and the softness in their gestures and legs are suggestive of the *demi-caractère* genre, with its specific qualities of grace and lightness in both style and steps. As can also be seen in the costume sketches by Louis-René Boquet for ballets by Noverre (see pp. 96 and 97), the differences here are very slight and are of "character", not rigor, inasmuch as both are perfectly framed in academic style.

The two pairs, *Paysans* (this page) and *Paysans Galants* (Gallant Peasants; top of next page), both by the same Jean-Baptiste Martin, do not escape from this tendency; and they are dressed in costumes made of precious and brightly-colored fabrics. But certain elements of their clothing, as well as the gestures and movements of their legs, recall a style of dancing that expresses exuberance and dynamism.
The context is no longer mythological, but rather one of a contemporary reality. This is a conventional setting that shuns verisimilitude, in favor of a generic elegance mixed with gallantry. The cap on the female *Gallant Peasant* figure on the opposite page, graciously placed on a sideward slant, and the richly embroidered apron both come across as charming, rather than being indications of belonging to a specific social class (the peasantry). The same goes for the costume of the female *Peasant* below, with its bodice with crossed laces, and the very finely-made apron.
In the young male *Paysans* (both galants and not), the youth's modern *redingote* and hat announce a contemporary setting with no reference to a rural context, contrary to what the title might seem to imply. In both male figures, an excellent balance is achieved between elegance and academism, represented by the ease of gesture and a fluency in the movements of the feet. The positioning of both youths' – their torsos slightly angled and knees bent – finds an equivalent in the maidens, who lift the hems of their aprons in a sign of exuberance. The only element differentiating the two versions – the *Paysan*, below, from that of the *Paysan Galant* on next page – apart from the latter's waistcoat, is in reference to the greater abundance of decorations in the gallant pair, in comparison to the "simplistic" peasants.
In both figures, In conclusion, this is a game similar to that of the nobility, when they dressed themselves up as *bergers*.

The standardization of costumes also influenced the Chinese characters reprinted here, who, in their gestures, costume construction and decorations, represent an extravagant and markedly Rococo-style compromise between "fashion" and references to an imaginary Chinese culture.
The female costume reprinted here (below) is in fact a modern dress, with charming flaps of fabric and "Chinese-style" headwear, worn by a model placed in a rather bizarre pose (legs bent, arms flexed alongside the body and hands turned upward), which will continue to be used in ballet as a distinctive mark of "Chinese" characters.
The male character wears a richly decorated jacket – a Western variation of the delicate Chinese surcoat.

These garments demonstrate the adaptation in French theater of traditional Oriental clothing (below, left). In the Western version of the "Oriental" suit (below, right), the long pantaloons are revealed under a garment that has been widened by a spacious *panier*. This is most likely a portrait of the actress Mme. Vestris (sister-in-law to Gaetano Vestris) in the role of Idamé in Voltaire's *L'Orphelin de la Chine*, reproduced in a print from 1778. Also at the playhouses, convention and luxury were both irremissible, and would be for quite some time, to the point of creating some quite unlikely hybrids.

The theater had its own rules, but it was quite different for portrait painting. In this painting from 1743 by Jacques-André-Joseph Aved, entitled *The Sultan's Wife in the Serraglio Gardens*, all of the elements that characterize "Turkish-style" costumes are present: the flowing dress, fur trimmings on the robe, and the fabric of pale-blue stripes on a lighter background. But only some of these same elements are to be found in the various costume sketches drawn in the mid-1700s. While Louis-René Boquet would respect also the sloping lines of the garment in his designs for Noverre's ballets (see p. 92, right), many costume designers *à la mode*, as we have seen, grafted these elements onto the existing canonic structure of women's dresses.

The Standardization of Costumes

These images of the *Trumpeter* and the *Faun*, datable to ca. 1740, attest to the process of abstraction incurred by the costume, both as a consequence of ballet's adjustment to fashion and as a result of a technical orientation that was moving toward a kind of virtuosity that revolved around itself. The *Faun*'s wild fur, placed elegantly over a *tonnelet* adorned with striking geometric decorations, has, by now, become a gallantly charming touch, in harmony with the extremely courteous and artificial gesture.

Flowery garlands for *Flora*, daggers and serpents for the *Fury* – these are the elements that essentially differentiate the two female costumes below, dating back to the mid-1700s. Notable in the skirt worn by the *Fury* are the angular shapes and the serpents, a symbol of evil that will still be present in the costumes for ballets by Noverre.

Love and Sensuality in French Art of the Early 1700s

This painting summarizes very efficiently the aesthetic trends in France during the 1730s and -40s. Gallant gestures, sweet gazes and, above all, a well-studied delicacy as regards the fabrics and styling of the costumes. These are the same qualities – softness, delicacy, elegance, gallantry and lightness – that marked the dancing style of the early 1700s.

Jean-Jacques de Troy, *The Declaration of Love*, 1731; Stiftung Preussische Schlösser und Gärten Berlin-Brandenburg

The Minuet – an Exaltation of Rococo Softness

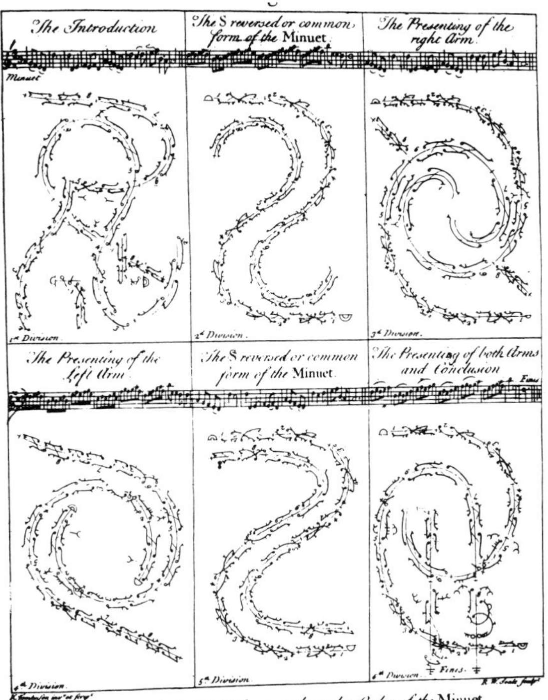

Introduced into lyric opera during the 1670s, the Minuet continued to be a symbol of the dominant aesthetics well into the mid-1700s, condensing within itself all the distinctive traits of Rococo taste (a predilection for sinuosity and softness, the use of oblique lines as a dynamic symbol), in a refined play of simulation, expressed through acts symbolic of the two central moments of love: courting and the encounter.
These can be seen in the second and third figures in the diagrams published by Kellom Tomlinson in *The Art of Dancing Explained by Reading and Figures*, printed in London in 1735.

In this detailing of the Minuet, the second of the six figures is a schematization of courting. The S-form represents the approach in space of two dancers, beginning in opposite corners (upper left and lower right), and their subsequent separation, resulting in an exchange of places.
The third figure is a diagram of union: the two dancers approach each other, offering right hands, and they complete a turn, hand-in-hand, before separating again.
The repetition in reverse of the two figures (see above) pays debt to the usual compositional symmetry of the era. The dance concludes with a joining of both hands, followed by a gesture of leave-taking.

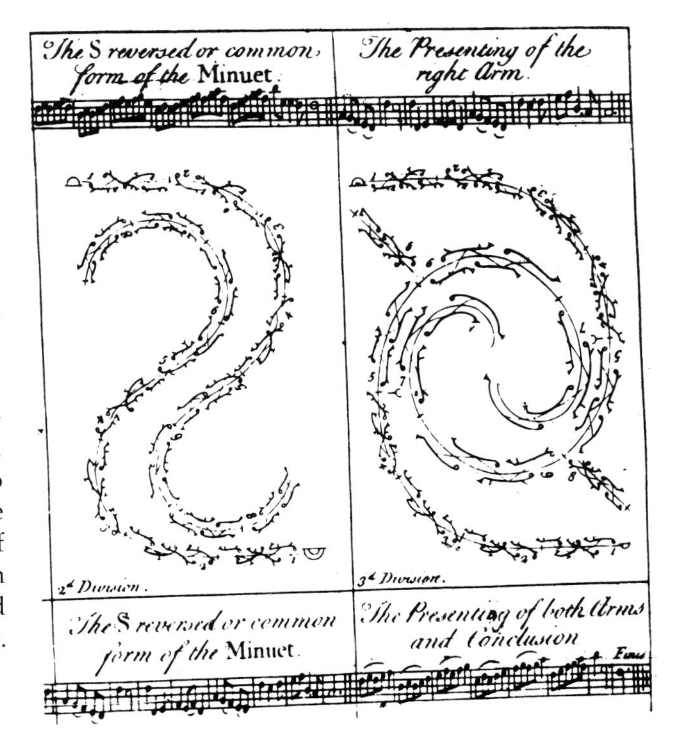

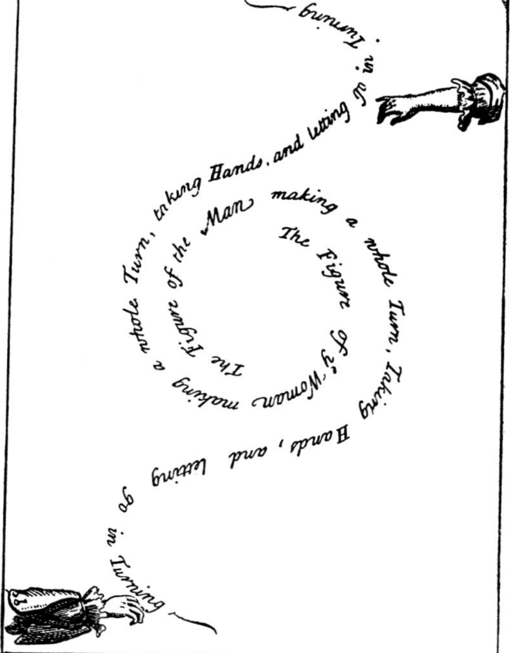

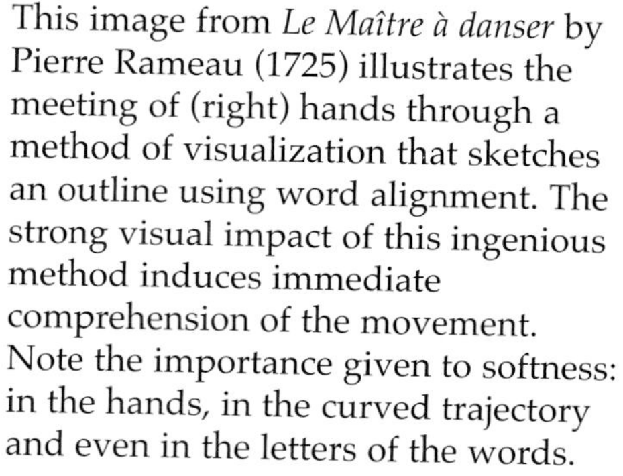

This image from *Le Maître à danser* by Pierre Rameau (1725) illustrates the meeting of (right) hands through a method of visualization that sketches an outline using word alignment. The strong visual impact of this ingenious method induces immediate comprehension of the movement. Note the importance given to softness: in the hands, in the curved trajectory and even in the letters of the words.

William Hogarth's *The Analysis of Beauty*, published in London in 1753, provides one of the most interesting testimonies as to the remarkable favor enjoyed by the Minuet in 18th-Century European society. Hogarth considered the Minuet an embodiment of beauty and grace, translated into undulating lines. In the image inserted into the frontispiece of *The Analysis of Beauty*, we see an S-shaped line (defined as a small serpent), as a sign of beauty that holds fickleness within.
The same undulating line appears in this self-portrait by Hogarth (1745, Tate Gallery, London), etched into the palette, where it is accompanied by the inscription, "line of beauty and grace".

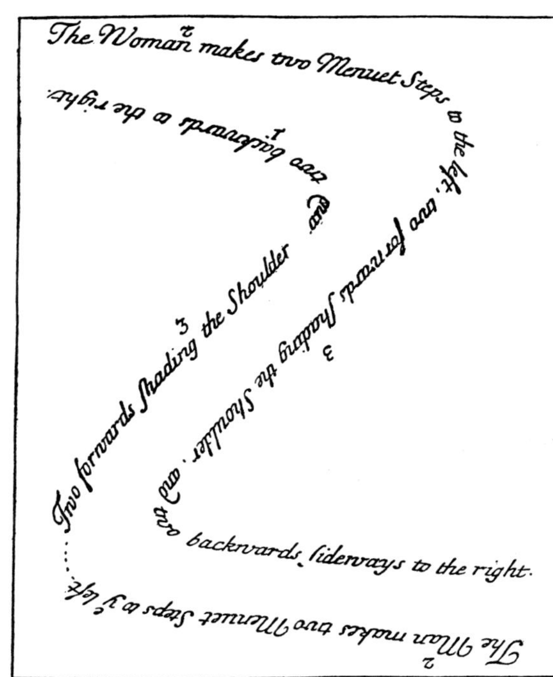

In Rameau's text (1725), we see that the "S" has been modernized and appears instead as a "Z". It is possible that the straightening out of the curved trajectory would have been influenced by the insistent presence (as regards both structure and position) of diagonals in Rococo paintings of gallant subjects. It is therefore possible that this transformation of "S" into "Z" derives from a need to mark the dance with a more eloquent sign of the newest trends.

In dance, the symbolic paths of the dancers and the symmetrical spatial composition did not allow for differentiation between male and female roles in the courting rituals so wonderfully reproduced in coeval painting.
As regards *The Declaration of Love* by Jean-François de Troy, from 1724, the Gentleman's forward thrust toward the Lady is made apparent by the row of buttons on the red redingote (the trajectory of which finishes at the tip of his shoe). This diagonal made by the buttons on the redingote is parallel to that on the dress of his beloved, who retreats, inclining away from him. One can recognize in this composition a diagonal similar to that drawn by Pierre Rameau for the second figure of the Minuet, using his typical method of visualizing words.

The Kiss, model by J. J. Kändler, ca. 1744. This Meissen porcelain statuette was inspired by the paintings of François Boucher, as were many others.

The Opéra-Comique Theater

Émile Campardon's text *Les Spectacles de la foire* (1877) summarizes the principal stages in the history of the *opéra-comique*, a peculiar type of performance, which, after having gone through various sorts of difficulties, finally managed to reconstitute and confirm itself as an autonomous form.
The term, which first appears in the 1710s but would only be consolidated around 1724, elucidates the nature of this type of performance, which included sections that were, in turn, recited, danced and sung – and even some vaudeville. Performances were organized on the occasions of the Saint-Germain and Saint-Laurent Fairs in Paris, to attract visitors and buyers to the stands that sold various types of articles within a wide range of value and price.
After a farraginous beginning, the Opéra-Comique theater would affirm its existence, making gains in both quality and originality; but rivalry with both the Comédie-Française and the Comédie-Italienne dictated its demise in 1745. This was to be only a temporary suspension, however, as activity restarted again in 1752 and continued to flourish until the fusion, in 1762, of the Opéra-Comique and the Comédie-Italienne. Among the most active and creative of its impresarios were Jean Monnet and the comedy playwright Charles-Simon Favart, two innovative promoters who were both deeply linked to the ballet.
The Opéra-Comique holds a role of primary importance in dance history for many reasons; among these are the Paris debut in 1726 of Marie Sallé (seen below in a 1732 portrait by Nicolas Lancret) and Jean-Georges Noverre's debut as a dancer in 1743, and then as a choreographer in 1754.

The Meaning of the Term "Ballet"

In the second volume of *Histoire du Théâtre de l' Opéra-Comique* by Jean-Augustin-Julien Deboulmiers, published in Paris in 1769, two types of performances at the Opéra-Comique can be distinguished, both of which were equally defined as *ballets*: one was a performance of prose, music and dance, and the other type contained only instrumental music and dance. The expression *ballet pantomime* also appears in the text. This was a mixed performance, in which the mimed sections were stylistically inspired by Italian Commedia dell'Arte.
Only in the second half of the 18th Century, and under the influence of the classical Restoration, would the term *ballet pantomime* also be used to denote an elevated lyric-choreographic form. In the same period, the term *pantomime noble* would be used to distinguish the popular pantomime of Italian origins from the pantomime of the dancer-actor in the new form of ballet with a narrative structure, the *ballet d'action*.
The image below contains a description of *Les Réjouissances flamandes* (Opéra-Comique, August 11, 1755), which, together with *Les Fêtes chinoises* (Opéra-Comique, July 1, 1754), launched the international career of Jean-Georges Noverre. In 1755, Noverre was invited to London by Garrick as *maître de ballets* at the Drury Lane Theatre.

486 *Hiſtoire du Théatre*

de leur Auteur, contenaient une critique aſſez ennuyeuſe de la Troupe de Franciſque & des piéces qu'elle repréſentait. Elles ſont les dernieres que donna Lalauze & ſa Troupe; & elles diſparurent après la troiſiéme repréſentation. Ces piéces ſont de Lafont; elles n'ont point d'extrait, & n'eurent aucun ſuccès.

LES RÉJOUISSANCES FLAMANDES.

Ballet.

11 Août 1755.

Voici l'idée de ce Ballet. Lorſque le rideau eſt levé, la décoration offre aux yeux du Spectateur un hameau. Une colline en forme le fond; elle eſt terminée par un grand arbre autour duquel ſont dreſſées des tables occupées par des Buveurs. Les deux côtés du Théatre ſont pareillement garnis de tables; & celles-ci ſont occupées par des Flamands & Flamandes qui boivent & ſe divertiſſent ſous des treilles. Le Groupe diſtingué

de l'Opéra Comique. 487

du Seigneur du lieu & de ſa famille richement habillés, eſt placé au milieu de la ſcène. Des Valets leur verſent à boire. Tandis que les Cabaretiers & les Cabaretieres ſervent, les Payſans & les Payſannes quittent leurs tables pour jouer à différens jeux. Ceux-ci ſe font peſer; ceux-là courent la bague, tandis que d'autres jouent à la boule & aux quilles. Un Vielleur & un Joueur de muſette leur font quitter leurs jeux, & les engagent à danſer. Le Ballet commence. Après pluſieurs entrées parriculieres & générales, le Seigneur du Village danſe un pas de quatre avec ſa famille, & enſuite un menuet. Les danſes ſont interrompues par une diſpute particuliere; mais, comme tous les hommes veulent s'en mêler, toutes les femmes font leurs efforts pour les en empêcher. Le Juge du lieu paraît & rétablit le calme. Le Ballet eſt terminé par une contredanſe générale, deſſinée d'une maniere nouvelle & piquante, exécutée par une foule prodigieuſe de Danſeurs & de Danſeuſes ſans embarras & ſans confuſion.

Xiv

Peasant Dances, Grotesque Dances and Pantomime in Early 18th-Century Italian Dance

During the 18th Century, Italian dance was widely appreciated and in demand in many European countries in a way comparable (though in lesser degree) to the work of the Italian architects and decorators who were invited to construct lavish residences and gardens for important aristocratic families.
From Tiberio Fiorilli, to whom is attributed the first importation of Italian Commedia dell'Arte into France and England (in 1635 and 1675, respectively), to Gaspero Angiolini, who became famous for his institution of reforms in Vienna in the early 1760s, various Italian artists were active in creating excellent performances and *divertissements* at the royal courts of Europe: Pietro Sodi in Paris, for example; the Balletti's in London; and Vincenzo Galeotti in Copenhagen, among others. These same artists cultivated a type of performance all across Europe that was radically different – in terms of style, theme and intent – from that of the French.
Traditional Italian dances covered quite a wide array of themes and movements, and they were often of a strongly humoristic nature. Daring and clownish capers were blended together with a pantomime that used very lively gestures; peasant dances or dances in diverse national settings were inserted into a picturesque framework, rich with humanity of a sort that was unheard of in French noble dancing. This type of performance took root across practically all of Europe between the end of the 17th Century and the beginning of the 18th, eventually creating its own autonomous realities, as well as an artistic lineage that would be carried forth among non-Italian artists.
One significant example of the transformation of these dances and their assimilation into a new international language that was in step with the times is the *divertissement* by Vincenzo Galeotti, a student of Angiolini, entitled *Les Caprices de Cupidon ou du maître de ballet*, the first performance of which took place on October 31, 1786, at the Royal Danish Theater. A version of this ballet was filmed in 1958, under the guidance of Danish balletmaster Hans Brenaa and set to a score by Jens Jolle. Despite the modifications perpetrated earlier by August Bournonville, as well as some further technical adjustments (Greeks dancing on pointe!), the ballet still reflects the hybridization and circulation of an "international" culture typical of the late 18th Century. It is a sort of light comedy, with a spirited and moralistic conclusion, presented to the public in a mischievous yet gracious way, in a style reminiscent of Molière or Italian playwright Carlo Goldoni. The finale is exhilarating, with couples of various "nationalities" – Tyrolean, Norwegian, Greek, French, Danish peasants, Quakers and three black African couples, as well – presenting themselves in their respective national dancing styles, before being united in matrimony at Cupid's temple in an amusing *coup de théâtre*.
Concrete and vivid evidence of the activities of the Italians abroad between the late 1600s and early 1700s is provided by Gregorio Lambranzi, author of the 1716 German-language text (with Italian translation) entitled *Neue und Curieuse Theatrialische Tantz-Schul* (New and Curious School of Theatrical Dancing). The publication, printed in Nuremberg by Johann Jacob Wolrab and illustrated with 101 copperplate engravings by Johann Georg Puschner, offers a cross-section of the activities by Italians at the "most prestigious theaters in Germany, Italy, France", as he writes on page 16 of the book.

The publication is a sort of sampling of dances, in which all the various types are represented: from the *danse grotesque* of slaves, prisoners, gypsies and drunkards, to rhythmical movements that take as their starting point the characteristic gestures of the various trades (blacksmith, seamstress, cooper, etc.); or further still, to little scenes placed in representative settings (of country boors, gardeners, soldiers or sailors).
The characters are inserted into scenic boxes delineated at the top by the musical score and at the bottom by a caption. The theater depicted is the one where such performances would generally have taken place – thus, a stage represented in reduced dimensions, with painted backdrops and wings that were functional and pertinent to the action.

Here to the left is the frontispiece from Gregorio Lambranzi's *Neue und Curieuse Theatrialische Tantz-Schul*, with the effigy of Minerva, who displays the first page leaf from *Loure pour deux hommes, dancée par Mr Blondy et Mr Philbois à l'Opéra de Scilla* by Louis Pécour, transcribed using a graphic system invented by Pierre Beauchamps. This was an explicit way of confirming the solid background in French dance attained by Lambranzi, a versatile and evidently cultivated artist.

In figure 29 from the first part of Lambranzi's book (below, left), *Harlequin* enters, dancing in his way, but *Scaramouche* enters as well, carrying a lantern...
In figure 35 (below, right), *Scapino* and his wife execute various steps, including *ballonnés, chassés, contretemps* and *pas de Rigaudon*, while wrenching their arms. At the end, back to back, they push at each other, and leave.

The scene in figure 6 from the same first part (below, left) presents a woman with a broom, who strikes her male companion and drives him away. This dance piece, writes Lambranzi, continues with the man's lively reaction, and it ends with a rather absurd dance.
In figure 7 (below, right), a man and woman threaten each other with large wooden plates, beating them together in time to the music, as the pair turns in a circle.

The trades offered a pretext for colorful dances filled with rhythm and humor. The images below are from the second part of Gregorio Lambranzi's book, and they show: four cooks, who, having entered from opposite sides, dance with long skewers in hand (no. 18, left); and two farriers forging a nail in time with the music (no. 25, right).

Figure 32 (left), also from the second part of the book, shows a dance that mimics a match of "lawn tennis" (a forerunner of today's tennis): as they dance, the two men hit the ball with their rackets in time to the music.

Figure 23 from the second part of Lambranzi's book and figure 8 from the first part show dances on the theme of love.
The couple in figure 23 (below, left) enter from the wings doing *ballonnés*. He kisses his own two fingers, places these kisses on the palm of his other hand, and blows them at the maiden's apron. She tries to put them inside her apron.
Figure 8 (below, right) shows a "peasant dance". Two lovers push at each other with their elbows and heels, while executing *contretemps* and *pas de Rigaudon* in a "peasant style". The elements that distinguish this as a peasant dance are quite clear: the beating of the heels on the floor, with upturned toes; the hands on the hips; the shoulder-to-shoulder positioning; and the traditional steps with origins in popular dances. Also notable is the display of grace that masks both technical skill and speed, but also serves as a mark of musicality – a grace that is far removed from that affected grace into which these dances would have been converted at the French court. We are, by now, very far removed from the dances of the *Paysan galant* (see pp. 56 and 57) – so courteous and steeped in artificiality – and we are similarly distant from the *effacements* of the Minuets (p. 30, top), despite the common folk origins.

A Cultivated Interpretation of the Popular World of the 1700s

As popular dances from the French provinces entered the court of Louis XIV, they were 'purified' of their coarser characteristics and enriched with refined arm movements. The same process of stylization characterized the production of porcelain statuettes at the factories in Meissen, Nymphenburg and Ludwigsburg in Germany, where popular characters, trades and stock characters from the Commedia dell'Arte were interpreted in refined decorative objects. However, even if the manufacturers' need to commercialize their products among the various classes – including the high-ranking – imposed a certain stylization of physical features, dress and gesture, if not an escape from realistic or slavish depictions, the designers (Johann Joachim Kändler in Meissen, Franz Anton Bustelli in Nymphenburg and Joseph Ness in Ludwigsburg) nevertheless did not deny their characters resolute portrayals, rendering their characterizations through the suggestive and highly communicative mobility of the body. In the images printed here, the positions are constructed upon twisted torsos, swinging hips and the contrast between the shoulders and gaze, all of which appears in plain opposition to the *aplomb* and "languissant" of French dance (as the *grotesque* dancer Gennaro Magri described it in 1779), represented below by the same Joseph Ness (right).

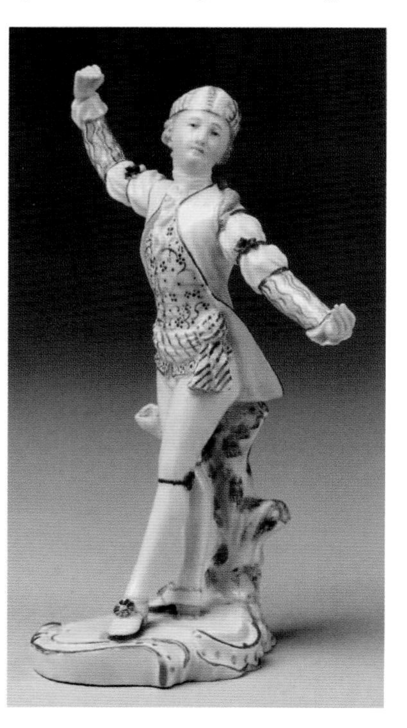

Researching a New Identity

François Boucher, *Pensent-ils au raisin?* (Are They Thinking about the Grape?), 1747; The Art Institute of Chicago. The inspirational source for this painting was the *opéra-comique* by Charles-Simon Favart, *Les Vendages de Tempé* (The Harvest in the Vale of Tempe), which would also have been seen by various choreographers during the second half of the 18th Century, among them Noverre.

Technical Advancement during the Mid-18th Century

Around the middle of the 18th Century, dance technique was to advance in surprising ways, due to the contribution of enterprising dancers who were anxious to impress their public with displays of technical bravura.
All of the elements instituted by Louis XIV that had inspired the Académie Royale de Danse had crystallized by now, and some of these same elements were even deformed in the process. This did not occur however with *aplomb* (the verticality of the torso) or with the counter-positioning of the legs and arms (opposition), as each of these would continue to fill the role of basic principle; but it did relate to the outward orientation of the feet. In a period of just a few decades, dance teachers would take the legs and feet, and open them to a full 180°, as a tangible symbol of a level of technical difficulty that could only be mastered through high professionalism and extensive exercise.
At the same time, among academic dancers, there were those who began to raise their legs toward the horizontal. Academic dance was now channeled into an increasingly specialized course that, in contrast to the basic rules drawn from classical art, already had little in common with salon dancing.

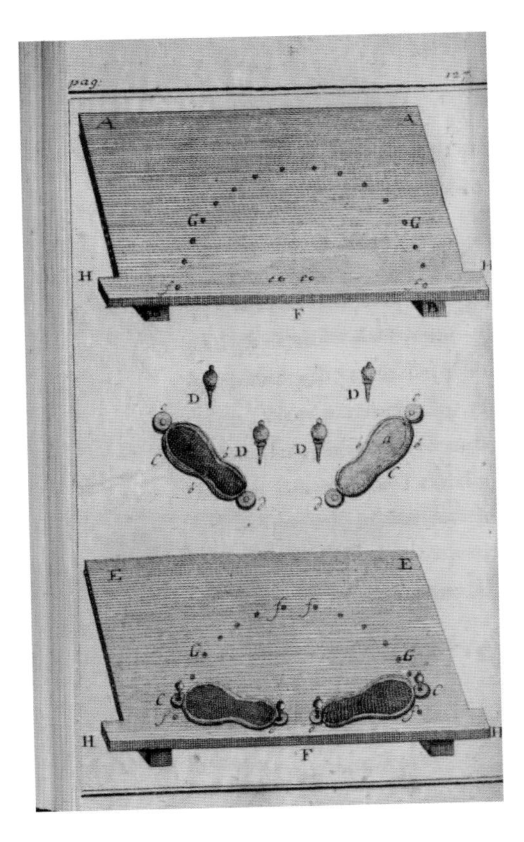

The machine called the "tourne-hanche", cited by Noverre in his *Lettres sur la Danse et sur les ballets* (1760, letter no. XII) and reproduced here from Charles-Hubert Méreau's *Réflexions sur le maintien et sur les moyens d'en corriger les défauts* (1760), was used during the mid-18th Century to increase the lateral deviation of the feet, that is, to force the outward rotation (*en-dehors*) of the entire limb, so as to place the soles of the feet in one continuous, lateral line. Noverre, though convinced of the need to increase the outward rotation, argued against this system, which he described as unnatural. Regardless of opinions regarding the validity, or not, of this clever device, the tablet represents indisputable evidence of the development of the *en-dehors*.

The Expansion of Movements in the 1760s

The engraving on the pre-frontispiece of Giovanni-Andrea Gallini's book, *A Treatise on the Art of Dancing*, edited in London in 1762 (single figure below), shows how the increased *en dehors* rotation in French ballet would be codified at the beginning of the 1760s and diffused all over Europe. It also testifies to a similar expansion in the movements of the arms, which now reach the level of the head, as a result of a general broadening of movement.
The influence of changes in taste and costumes is evident here; but the conditioning by practices common in the social dancing of the bourgeois class is nevertheless not to be underestimated.

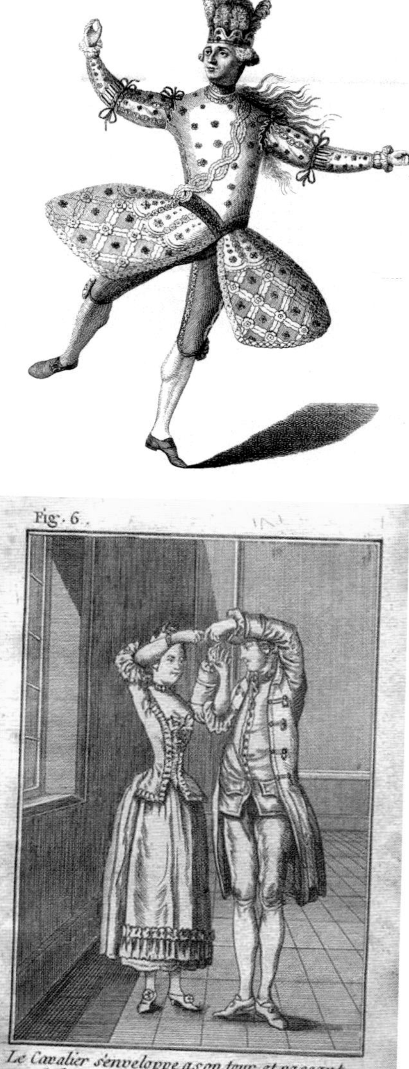

Both the figure of the *Allemande* (lower left), from the treatise by Guillaume entitled *Caractères de la danse Allemande* (ca. 1769) and the pair of Neapolitan earthenware figurines in similar poses, from the second half of the 18th Century (lower right), show arms that are raised, crossed and entwined high and behind the body, which not only increases the breadth of the arm movements, but also brings the bodies closer together.

Notable in these two porcelain figurines from the Residenzschloss in Ludwigsburg, which were designed by Joseph Ness and date back to around 1765, is the erect and rather stiff position of the bodies, which is typical of French academic dance in the early 1760s. The chests are very much opened by a pronounced lowering of the shoulders and the retraction of the abdomen, and the poses are composed and gracious: the side arms are extended and slightly raised, and the heads, delicately inclined to the side, are held in an elegant attitude which, by the end of the century, would come to be known as *abandon*. This is clearly a display of pure academic style, and considering the embellishments and fashioning of the costumes, it is presumably of *demi-caractère* nature – a contemporary setting in the figure on the right, while the figure on the left displays an academic "*pastoral-galant*" style, with the *tonnelet* decorated with a characteristic segmented sash.

Another important element is the positioning of the figures and their relationship to space.

In the iconography of the late 17th Century and first quarter of the 18th, figures are positioned according to academic rules, and the head and gaze generally accompany – "in opposition" – the raised gesture of the arm, as if this were an integral part of the body's general equilibrium. The gaze is accompanied by a slight *abandon*, conferring grace and nobility upon the figure (see p. 28).

The positioning in these figurines, on the other hand, follows a logic that is substantially different: the gaze is directed at the spectator and is turned toward the same direction as the arm that is opened to the side. This implies two choices: a) regarding the figure's "presentation", a reference to the public is regarded as obligatory, and b) the position more highly favored here is with the legs crossed and the arms "open" in respect to the public, which, in the 19th Century, will be defined as *croisé*.

Technical Observations

The images on this page and the next are taken from the eleven volumes given by Jean-Georges Noverre to Stanislaw II August of Poland in 1766, presently conserved at the University of Warsaw Library. The images are contained, specifically, in the penultimate of the five volumes (VII-XI) that bring together costume sketches drawn by Louis-René Boquet for Noverre's ballets.
The figures portray a *Triton* and a *Roman*; and the absence of reference to specific ballets leads to the conclusion that they are generic character types. Both costume sketches nevertheless date back to the productive years when Noverre worked at the court of Karl Eugen von Württemberg (1760-1766).
Note the general orientation of the body, the direction of the gaze, and the relation between the upper part of the body (arms, chest and head) and the lower part (i.e. legs). Both figures assume an oblique position. In the figure on the left (*Triton*), however, the position is built upon a decisive counter-positioning of the upper and lower parts of the body and the superimposing of one leg over the other, which results in their appearing crossed (in *croisé*). The arms do not respect canonical opposition to the legs, inasmuch as this is impeded by the gesture of lifting the seashell. The gaze deviates toward the side of the raised hand, creating at the same time a rapport with the spectator.
The pose of the figure on the right (*Roman*), on the other hand, is extraordinarily similar to 19h-Century *effacé*, as regards the arms, body and positioning of the head. Opposition between the legs and arms is respected; the chest is only slightly angled, leaving both shoulders in view.

Zb. król. vol. 804 – k. 46

Zb. król. vol. 804 – k. 49

In this figure of an *Ondin* from Noverre's ballet *Renaud et Armide*, the position in *croisé* does follow the rules, even though the gaze is lowered. The position is analogous to that of the *Triton* on the preceding page and also exhibits a canonical counter-positioning between arms and legs. The legs are rotated outward (*en dehors*), as prescribed by the norms. The opposing arm is raised to the level of the head.

Zb. król. vol. 802 – k. 53

This figure of a *Naiad* from the same ballet *Renaud et Armide* is extremely interesting not only for the positioning of the body in relation to space – sacrificed in order to draw attention to the costume – but also for the placement of the hands, which clearly indicates that this character has a dancing role. The thumb and index finger of the left hand are drawn together, while the other fingers are opened elegantly; the right hand takes a position that resembles the styles of the 1800s (see p. 189). Note the richly decorated costume, preciously elaborated with embroidery and inlays of simulated seashells, seaweed and coral, and the delicate leaf necklace and gracious headdress of seaweed and coral. And finally, observe the shoe, with its small heel.

Zb. król. vol. 802 – k. 54

The Birth of *Pantomime Noble* and the *Ballet d'Action*

In the first half of the 18th Century, the term "pantomime" was generally used to refer to an act that was silent, but highly expressive, as was practiced by Italian actors in the parodies and burlesque adventures of Harlequin, Columbine and other stock characters with Commedia dell'Arte origins, or in the lively exploits of various other character types (farmers, craftsmen, etc.).
Hence, in the first half of the 18th Century, the category *pantomime* included all that which, through the use of gesture, steps and movements, either expressed a state of mind (feelings, thoughts and memories) or described any "sort of thing" (objects, people, situations, etc.), using the conventional gestural codes inherited from Italian theater.
In France, the pantomime inherited from the Commedia dell'Arte was the soul of many performances at the Opéra-Comique and Comédie-Italienne, and in the first half of the 18th Century, pantomime enjoyed notable growth all across Europe.

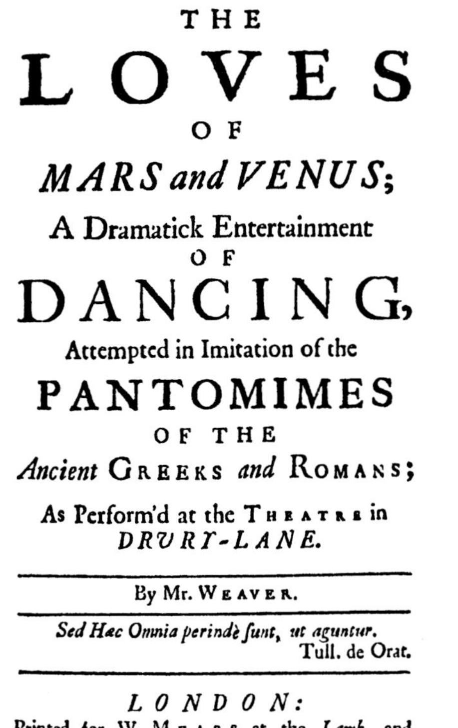

THE
LOVES
OF
MARS and VENUS;
A Dramatick Entertainment
OF
DANCING,
Attempted in Imitation of the
PANTOMIMES
OF THE
Ancient GREEKS *and* ROMANS;
As Perform'd at the THEATRE in
DRURY-LANE.

By Mr. WEAVER.

Sed Hæc Omnia perindè sunt, ut aguntur.
Tull. de Orat.

LONDON:
Printed for W. MEARS at the *Lamb*, and J. BROWNE at the *Black-Swan*, without *Temple-Bar*. M DCC XVII. Price 6 *d.*

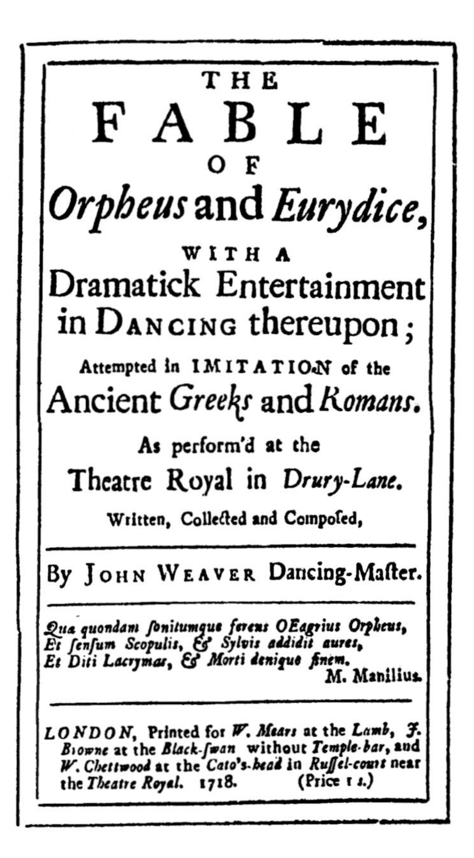

THE
FABLE
OF
Orpheus and *Eurydice*,
WITH A
Dramatick Entertainment
in DANCING thereupon;
Attempted in IMITATION of the
Ancient *Greeks* and *Romans*.
As perform'd at the
Theatre Royal in *Drury-Lane.*
Written, Collected and Composed,

By JOHN WEAVER Dancing-Master.

Qua quondam sonitumque ferens OEagrius Orpheus,
Et sensum Scopulis, & Sylvis addidit aures,
Et Diti Lacrymas, & Morti denique finem.
M. Manilius.

LONDON, Printed for *W. Mears* at the *Lamb*, *J. Browne* at the *Black-swan* without *Temple-bar*, and *W. Chetwood* at the *Cato's-head* in *Russel-court* near the *Theatre Royal*. 1718. (Price 1 *s.*)

The two posters reproduced on the preceding page, announcing performances created by the English choreographer John Weaver for the Drury Lane Theatre in London in 1717 and 1718, respectively, testify to the experimentation of an artist whose roots lie in the world of English pantomime. Here, Weaver wanted to utilize both the language of gestures and the scenographic tools from pantomime performances to stage tales such as *The Loves of Mars and Venus* or *The Fable of Orpheus and Eurydice*, in a sort of "dramatick entertainment in Dancing" (*ballet d'action*), intended as an idealized imitation of ancient Greek and Roman pantomime. This experiment provides evidence of a general interest in the art of pantomime from ancient Greek and Roman theater, which, even prior to the 1750s, was drawing the attention of artists and the lettered. Documentation on ancient theater provided the stimulus for new developing perspectives and promoted innovative experimentation, not only in dance, but also in dramatic theater. From this, the *pantomime noble* was born: a novel language of gesture used for epic and tragic plots in the new ballets of narrative structure.

During the 1740s and -50s, *pantomime noble* was the subject of experimentation by various artists: from the Austrian Franz Anton Hilverding to the Dutchman Jean-Baptiste Dehesse, and, from 1761 on, also the Florentine Gaspero Angiolini, founder of the so-called Italian School. At the same time, but under totally different suppositions, the future flag-bearer of what would come to be known as the French line, Jean-Georges Noverre, began to stir. Both Angiolini and Noverre used pantomime to build a new form of ballet performance, which would henceforth be designated as *ballet d'action* (or *en action*), or *ballet pantomime*, in which the word "pantomime" refers either to that of ancient theater or to the *pantomime noble*. Noverre's pantomime, in particular, was inspired by the more modern and advanced line of French theatrical tragedy and that of the Englishman David Garrick.

The mimic style invented by Noverre was characterized by a strong accentuation of gestures and a raw realism that had the effect of striking deep chords within the spectator, provoking intense emotions among the public.

Despite the rarity of iconographic documentation, it is possible, as we will see on the following pages, to deduce certain essential traits of the mimic style created by Noverre and employed by his disciples in the *ballets d'action* from the early second half of the 18th Century.

Iconographic Documentation

One precious piece of documentation of *pantomime noble* in the 1760s is the gouache below by Carmontelle (artist's name for Louis Carrogis) illustrating a suggestive moment in the *pas de deux pantomime* from the opera *Sylvie*, which was staged in 1765. The dancers portrayed are Marie Allard and Dauberval (the stage name adopted by Jean Bercher), who, from 1757, was a faithful disciple of Noverre and interpreter of his choreography.
As Noverre emphasizes, Dauberval, going against the trends, had the courage to present himself unmasked, using a mime language that had been rejected until that time at the Paris Opera. In this gouache, which was reproduced as a print by Jean-Baptiste Tilliard in 1767 (p. 83), Dauberval is portrayed in a gallant courting attitude. Marie Allard (as a *Nymph* from Diana's retinue) resists the young *Hunter*'s advances, as he signals his intention to convince her. Comparing the gesture of the woman in this *pas de deux* with that of the French actress Mademoiselle Dumesnil in the scene from Voltaire's *Sémiramis* pictured on the opposite page, Noverre's source of inspiration is confirmed to be the acting styles of both the Englishman David Garrick and the Frenchman Lekain, portrayed on the opposite page together with Dumesnil in this English print from 1772.

The devotion of young Dauberval (he was just 24) to the style of his teacher Noverre is to be gathered from other details, as well. His costume, for example, has no *tonnelet*, but rather a slightly puffy short skirt, decorated in a "gallant" style with garlands and bows, as in many of the costumes designed by Louis-René Boquet for Noverre's ballets (see p. 103, right). Similarly, the dress worn by the danseuse is light and somewhat wide at the hips, and it is enlivened by the asymmetrical surcoat and the garland that slants across her breast, which is rather similar to that of Noverre's *Bacchante* on page 103.
The "beautiful disorder" championed by Noverre is to be noted in both costumes, as well as the prominence given to the diagonal (in the attitudes and positioning of the two dancers), symbol *par excellence* of asymmetry. The bodies of the two dancers divaricate in like manner, forming two oblique lines. But the differing positioning of the legs demonstrates that their intentions are indeed divergent. The lady's feet are placed in such a way as to indicate a step away, which, if taken together with the attitude of her arms and face, can be interpreted as refusal. He, on the other hand, although bending away from his beloved, seems to have just taken a step toward the maiden, while, at the same time, making a gesture of amorous conviction.
Indeed, the caption under Tilliard's print reads: "On her dignity does the Nymph repose, / her lover already losing hope of moving her; / yet she looks toward him as she dreams of flight. / Nymph who dreams of the torments she causes / the moment to heal them approaches."

Pantomime in Sources from the Applied Arts

Another very interesting source of iconography relating to pantomime of the early 1760s is the porcelain manufactured in Ludwigsburg, already cited in the preceding chapter. The specific reference here is to one *pas de deux pantomime* and a *pas de trois pantomime* with one *danseuse* and two *danseurs*. The dating of these figurines (1760 and 1763, respectively) would support the supposition of Joseph Ness having been inspired by some ballet by Noverre, who was indeed working in Stuttgart and Ludwigsburg during this period, at the service of Duke Karl Eugen von Württemberg. The *tonnelet*, however, and indeed the entire assembly of the women's costumes – and at the same time, the absence of any comprehensive documentation about Noverre's ballets of the early 1760s in Stuttgart – all encourage a suspension of judgment on this point, so we shall limit ourselves to a few observations and considerations.
All of the characters portrayed in these statuettes have their faces covered in a very heavy makeup base, as was usual in the theater, with copious rouge on their cheeks, as can also be seen in Boquet's sketches. The costumes are assembled in a manner standard for ballet performances – a wide *tonnelet* for the male dancers and skirts with an ovoid structure (held up by *paniers*) for the women – with the exception of the ladies' hems, which are raised to nearly halfway up the calf. In the *pas de trois*, the head plumes and the segmented, colored bands on the men's costumes are elements typical of French ballet's *demi-caractère* genre. In the *pas de deux*, the man's wig, and the female character's hairstyling tend to suggest a comedy based on contemporary themes.

Further to the figures on the preceding page, one can see how the schematic gestures in the dancers reproduced in porcelain pair up nicely with the unnatural placement of the legs, which, especially in the couple on the left, are forced to the 180° *en-dehors* of academic ballet.
The attitudes taken by the characters would suggest possible disputes between lovers. In the trio, the two young lovers are thrust into each other's arms, in the presence of a slighted would-be lover. In the duo, a maiden rejects the propositions of her escort, a subject widely used in Rococo painting (see de Troy's painting on p. 63).
What is striking is the positioning of the maiden, drawing one hand to her face, while her torso is forcefully inclined in the direction opposite to that of her beloved. This removal away from the perpendicular, assuming an oblique body position, was an obligatory mode in the actor's art for demonstrating interior conflict (see page 203).
A similar attitude is recognizable in this satirical print (below) of Giovanna Baccelli, Gaetano Vestris and Adelaïde Simonet in Noverre's ballet *Jason and Medea*, restaged in London by the same Vestris in 1781.

Dancing Female Harlequin with Mask, designed by J. J. Kändler for the Meissen factory, 1764; Historisches Museum Basel, Pauls-Eisenbeiss-Stiftung

The *Ballet d'Action*

Portrait of Jean-Georges Noverre by Jean-Baptiste Perronneau, n.d.;
Musée de l'Opéra de Paris.

The Use of Space in the *Ballet d'Action*, Substantiated by Franz Anton Hilverding

One of the rare pieces of evidence of a *ballet d'action* scene from the mid-1700s is this drawing by Bernardo Bellotto, which dates back to 1759. The print reproduces a scene from Franz Anton Hilverding's pantomime ballet *Le Turc généreux*, premiered in Vienna in April, 1758, to honor the visit of the Turkish envoy.
Observing the scene in its entirety, one can grasp the elements relating to the structure of the theater, the lighting and the stage scenery, on the one hand, and to the composition of the action and the concept of utilizing expressive gesture, on the other. Chandeliers hang above the forestage, illuminating the frontal area of the stage only. The stage space in which the dancers move is limited in depth, so that most of the action occurs downstage. Nevertheless, a painted backdrop with a central tunnel of trees – at the end of which, the vision is drawn into a maritime scene with seafaring vessels – creates the effect of breaking through into spatial profundity.
As regards the action, one notices a strong dynamism in the bodies and gestures. Men and women run across the stage from left to right, converging on the center-stage, where the main action occurs. Although their gestures and also their numbers are proportioned (i.e., balanced), the two groups move from different points in the space: the women from the side, and the men from the upstage corner, thus creating, through disparity, a dynamism that accords with the action of the central group. This latter group (four characters) moves cross-wise from upstage to down-, toward the proscenium, with a progression of height that leads from the full standing figure down to the figure in a kneeling position with the body bent to the side. And all of the figures have open arms. Thus, the dramatic content is communicated not only through gesture, but is also played out through a spatial composition of veiled asymmetry and oblique lines.

Jean-Georges Noverre's *Ballet d'Action*

Noverre's fame is connected to the publication of his theoretic text *Lettres sur la Danse et sur les Ballets* (Lyon-Stuttgart, 1760), in which the artist promotes a substantial reform of French theatrical dancing, illustrating his aesthetic line and main conceptual cruxes. Nonetheless, it is with his production of innovative choreography that he would succeed in making radical inroads that affected ballet's historical course and create that flock of disciples who would transmit his teachings to subsequent generations of the 19th Century.

His activities unfolded over a span of more than half a century, touching some of the most famous European courts (Stuttgart, Vienna, London, Paris and Milan), where he created hundreds of ballets, dances and *divertissements*. His collaborators, as regards music, were the orchestra conductors (Johann Joseph Rodolphe, Florian Johann Deller, Joseph Starzer and Franz Aspelmayr), while for the scenery, he depended on the contributions of talented stage designers like Innocente Colomba and Giovanni-Niccolò Servandoni. For the costumes, Noverre enjoyed the good fortune provided by his continuous collaboration with the clever Louis-René Boquet (student of the painter François Boucher), who embellished his ballets for some thirty years.

Inspired by the ideals of the Enlightenment and aligned with the most advanced trends in visual arts and literature, the process begun by Noverre was urged forward by the need to re-qualify dance as a form that would represent human vicissitudes and feelings, and to return to the body its inherent expressive and communicative potential. In those years, a concept of dance was being asserted that saw it as an imitative art equal to poetry and painting (as can be seen in the writings of Charles Batteux [1746] and Louis de Cahusac [1754]); and the condemnations against academic ballet, with its abstract but conventional geometry of steps and gestures that impeded the unfurling of the interpreters' expressive capacities, were growing in number. These were also the years during which the "imitation of nature", the founding aesthetic principle of the imitative arts, was developing a new meaning: the expression of feelings and passions – which combined quite well with that "natural" disorder so wonderfully represented in classical art and Rococo paintings. So this was the fundamental lever that propelled Noverre to interpose the experimental path that would lead him to create the *ballet d'action* and, with this, to the costume reform that began with the elimination of the mask in 1757.

Verity of gesture and verisimilitude as regards the stage settings and costumes were the aesthetic principles that would guide him in his arrangement of large composite 'frescoes', in which the dancers' movements linked up with the other performance elements (music, stage design and costume) in a sort of "total" theater.

To surprise, move and amaze the public – these were among the main objectives of his ballets, for which the "sources of the action", whether lovable, painful, hedonistic or wicked, all had to be impressive and suggestive. To this end, Noverre resorted to some uncommon compositional tools and stage devices: carriages emerging from the waves, coaches rising to the heavens, palaces consumed by flames; terrifying voices that burst out onto the stage and suggestive silences that sliced through the music; and a picturesque asymmetry in the choreographic arrangements and costumes – all these were used in order to involve the spectator and strike deeply at his or her emotions.

For the sections of *la danse proprement dite* (pure dance), Noverre followed the same criteria, and this is why, in order to restore dramatic significance to the dance and integrate it fully into the action, he re-calibrated the presence of dance in ballet, choosing in each case the most appropriate style and reformulating the academic sections in such a way as to escape the hollow "pleasure for the eyes" that had characterized the traditional academic ballets.
It was this choice, above and beyond his creation of a new language of passionately expressive gestures, that placed Noverre's artistic proposition in clear contrast to the practices of the Paris Opera, which had for decades hinged upon a system that imposed onto dance an abstract and symbolic geometry based upon complexity and conventional rigor.
The subjects of Noverre's ballets were quite varied, but a large number of these, following the trends in tragic theater of the period, were garnered from ancient history and, in particular, from mythological sources. This was a choice of principle, inasmuch as Noverre compared "his" ballet to epic poetry, with its fantastical characters and the possibility to travel through space and time.
The images to follow are from the collection of costume sketches given by Noverre in 1766 to Stanislaw II August of Poland, now preserved at the University of Warsaw Library, and from the second of two volumes offered by the artist to Gustav III of Sweden in 1791.
The sketches have been organized and ordered into a sampling that highlights some of the theoretic aspects and fundamental aesthetics of Noverre's reform: truth, verisimilitude, symbolism inspired by classical iconography, communicative functionality and character recognition through the costuming, and a rapport with the prevailing styles. In some of these sketches, it is also possible to extract some technical and stylistic data that underscore the importance attributed by Noverre to *la danse proprement dite* (pure dance) and to technique, despite the invectives contained in his *Lettres*.
Also included are images of the distinctive dances of certain national settings and dances of a caricatured *grotesque* style.

Experimentation by Noverre in the 1750s

Ut pictura poesis (as painting, so is poetry), that is, the comparing of art forms, stands as one of the founding principles of Noverre aesthetics. Basing his argument on Plutarch, he compares dance with both painting and poetry. To Noverre, ballet, in its visual construction, is a painting, and in the conception of adventure and action, it is a poem. But painting always occupies the first row in his eyes, so much so that his ballets of the 1740s and early 1750s can be described as moving paintings.

Les Fêtes chinoises (The Chinese Feasts), staged at the Saint-Laurent Fair in Paris on July 1, 1754, is one of the first ballets in this genre. The two costume sketches here, below, from the tenth volume of the collection at the University of Warsaw Library, can be attributed to this work. From chronicles of the era, we can deduce how Noverre would have attempted to render the realistic setting; but from these sketches, one comprehends just how much he would be forced to concede to the luxury imposed both by the theater and by the stylistic extravagance in this period.

The two subjects reprinted here represent clearly contrasting character types: the *Mandarin*, caricatured and ungainly, with a *grotesque* bearing that is garishly accentuated by the mask; and the *Chinoise*, delicate and affable, and dressed in an elegant, precious suit. Comparing these sketches to the characters from the painting reproduced on the opposite page, entitled *La Pêche chinoise* (Chinese Fishing), by the famous Rococo artist François Boucher, let us observe the female character more closely. Her hair adornments and long bloomers are identical to those worn by the lady in Boucher's painting. The upper part of the costume is, however, different from Boucher's version: the long robe from the painting is replaced by a richly decorated garment, which is partially covered by an equally precious jacket. Evident in this solution is Boquet's proposal to satisfy the principle of verisimilitude supported by Noverre, but without renouncing the "spectacular" requirements that were imposed by ballet of the era. The result is a variegated and luxurious reworking in theatrical chords of "Chinese" dress, in which the "beautiful disorder" championed by Noverre finds a joyous and radiant application in pure Rococo style.

Zb. król. vol. 804 – k. 087

Zb. król. vol. 804 – k. 088

La Pêche chinoise is the painting by the famous Rococo artist François Boucher for *La Tenture chinoise* (The Chinese Parament), one of ten sketches commissioned by the Beauvais manufactory in 1742 and now preserved at the Musée des Beaux-Arts in Besançon.
As we have seen, Noverre and Louis-René Boquet took strong cues from these sketches for the action, scenery and costumes of the ballet *Les Fêtes chinoises*.
Note in this painting the "beautiful disorder" so praised by Noverre in his theoretic writings.

This engraved reproduction of the famous painting *Les Réjouissances flamandes* (The Flemish Feasts) by David Teniers le Jeune (1648) provides a sort of preliminary documentation of the ballet of the same title, which Noverre staged on August 11, 1755, at the Saint-Laurent Fair in Paris. Although Noverre re-balanced and re-centered it, the scenery for the ballet nevertheless faithfully reproduces the Flemish canvas, so much so that the critics gave Noverre's creation the nickname "Teniers dansé".
The description of this ballet written by Desboulmiers in the second volume of his *Histoire du théâtre de l'Opéra Comique* from 1769 (see p. 66) is recognizable in Teniers' painting: a group of ladies and gentlemen dancing the Minuet (on the right) and the set tables around which the peasants entertain themselves, drinking and merrymaking.

The Academic Genres in Costumes from Noverre's Ballets

As we have seen, from the first half of the 18th Century until its end, academic dance was rigidly divided into three *genres*: the *sérieux*, the *demi-caractère* and the *comique*. The *demi-caractère* genre was also known as *galant-pastoral*. The *sérieux* had, as alternatives terms, *noble* and *héroïque*, the latter signifying of high rank and generally implying a setting from antiquity.
In his 1760 publication *Lettres sur la Danse et sur les Ballets* (letter no. IX), Noverre describes the dancers of the three categories.

> The genius of each of the three dancers who take up these particular styles should be as different as their statures, their features and their studies. One should be grand, the other gallant, and the last amusing… The stature suitable for a dancer in the *sérieux* style is, without question, noble and elegant… For the *demi-caractère* genre and for voluptuous dancing, a medium stature is undoubtedly that which is proper, for this can unite of all the beauties of an elegant stature. Of what importance is height, if beautiful proportions shine equally over all parts of the body? The stature of the *comique* dancer requires less perfection; the shorter he be, the more his body will afford grace, gentility and naiveté to his expression.

Noverre does not limit himself to observations on physical conformity and dancing style, but rather develops the classification by comparing these genres to those found in poetry and painting, which he considered sister arts to dance. So, the *sérieux* is compared to tragic theater and historical painting; the *demi-caractère* genre is set alongside the *commedia* and those refined paintings of Rococo-inspired *galant-pastoral* subjects, in particular, the works of François Boucher. In his *Lettres*, Noverre unites the *comique* and the *grotesque* into one genre – as dual, complementary aspects of one style, which is likened to second rate *commedia* and to the so-called "genre painting", above all that of the celebrated Flemish painter David Teniers le Jeune.
It must be noted, however, that such classifications derive from Noverre's pre-1760 experiences. In observing his ballets from the period when he was working at the courts at Stuttgart and Vienna (1760-1766 and 1767-1774), one notices that the map of genres was better articulated. This can be deduced in detail from the costume sketches drawn by Louis-René Boquet in the early 1760s and given by Noverre to Stanislaw II August of Poland in 1766.
Looking at volume X of the eleven volumes now preserved at the University of Warsaw Library, it can be clearly deduced that diverse character types belong to the *sérieux* genre: certain divinities with their followers (for example, *Juno*, with *Sylphs* and *Sylphides*), allegories (such as Earth), and the *Bergers* and *Bergères héroïques*. The *comique* genre, together with the *demi-caractère*, on the other hand, embraces characters that range from *Grape Harvesters* and *Fauns*, to *Pastres* and *Pastourelles*. Characters with *grotesque* traits and exaggerated gestures also appear, like the *Mandarin* (see p. 92, left) and the personifications of evil sentiments (see p. 106).

The Sérieux *Genre*

According to the classicist traditions of decorum, a dancer of the *sérieux* genre has a simple, elegant style and is distinguished by broad and measured movements that exalt the statuesque beauty of the body, that is, the harmony of its proportions and the perfection of line with which the classical concept of beauty is identified: beauty as harmony and perfection.
However, as we see in these costume sketches by Boquet from the early 1760s (volumes VIII and X), the calmness of the gestures in the *sérieux* dancer and the composure of the movements do not disown the "gracious" effect, which is rendered with flowers, bows and garlands, and accentuated with richly feathered plumes on the head: wide and ostentatious for the men, only slightly intimated for the women. The inevitable garland, the bows and also the segmented bands in the male costume all have gallant connotations. The garland is also recognized to be a "chain of love".

Zb. król. vol. 802 – k. 104

Zb. król. vol. 804 – k. 04

Zb. król. vol. 804 – k. 20

Zb. król. vol. 804 – k. 19

The Demi-Caractère *Genre*

The costume sketch below, left, from volume X of the collection in Warsaw, shows the basic characteristics of the *demi-caractère*. The other two costume sketches from the same volume, and the group of porcelain figures below, designed by Joseph Ness in 1765 for the factory in Ludwigsburg, show variants of the *demi-caractère* genre. Instead of the typical *tonnelet*, the male dancer wears breeches in a modern style that suggest a contemporary theme. Comparable costumes are found on the peasants in the porcelain *pas de trois*, even if their fashioning is less lavish and spectacular than was obligatory at the Paris Opera.
In sum, one gathers that the distinctive traits of the *demi-caractère* genre are grace and lightness, technically expressed as elasticity, dexterity and quickness, while in the clothing, a greater mobility can be discerned as regards the draping and colors.

Zb. król. vol. 804 – k. 71

Zb. król. vol. 804 – k. 79

Zb. król. vol. 804 – k. 80

Zb. król. vol. 804 – k. 82

Zb. król. vol. 804 – k. 59

The **Comique** *Genre*

The three images placed together on this page for comparison show how the character of the *pâtre* (shepherd) was portrayed around the mid-18th Century. Note the similarity between the male costume sketch (above, left, from vol. X) and the subject in this Meissen statuette from 1755 (right), designed by E. F. Meyer, which portrays an elegant shepherd as he shears his sheep. The gesture and elements representative of the character's clothes (wide-brimmed hat, thick shoes and the informal clothing) unequivocally project the young shepherd into a rural setting, while the accuracy as regards the garments, the representative manner of the subject and the refined workmanship all betray a cultivated vision of a popular subject.

The shepherdesses drawn by Boquet for Noverre's ballets, also during the years 1760-1766, present similar characteristics, even if this character's bearing is more obviously elegant and courteous (see above, right, from vol. X). Her bodice, dainty apron and petite jacket all imply a contemporary setting, while the numerous bows spread throughout the costume suggest an academic dancing style, even if interpreted in a more technically dynamic manner and with a more fluent use of gesture.

The Grotesque *Genre*

In these costume sketches by Louis-René Boquet for *Ballet Chinois* (the *Mandarin*) and *Médée* (*Vengeance*), from volumes X and VII, respectively, one can infer that such characters could not have belonged to the academic genres. The faces, covered by masks, and bodies are rendered in caricature and in *grotesque*, and the same applies to the gestures – emphatic and disheveled. In the system of classification of the second half of the 18th Century, in fact, the *grotesque* constituted its own genre, separate from the academic classifications.
In the costume sketch on the right, it is also interesting to note how the concept of the 'terrific' (that which terrifies) from classical iconography and late 17th-Century ballet would live on in Noverre's ballets.

Zb. król. vol. 804 – k. 87

Zb. król. vol. 801 – k. 013

Characters in Noverre's Ballets

Divinities

The following two examples testify as to the ways in which Noverre, and consequently his designer Boquet, represented the divinities. Although the costume sketch collections in both Warsaw and Stockholm include ample and varied representations of divinities, the selection here has been guided by a desire to underscore the symbolic function of both costumes and positioning.
Sumptuous clothing, crown and scepter, and dignified gestures all place the characters' regal natures in relief. In the costume sketch for *Pluto*, the high, plumed headdress is consistent with the presence of the light cape, while the elegant bow at the waist confers a worldly touch to the somber costume and substantially decreases the symbolic weight of the infernal flame that appears on the bodice.
The clouds and peacock feathers on sky-blue setting that adorn *Juno*'s costume are clear references to the role of sky goddess attributed to her by Noverre in *The Judgment of Paris*. Clouds and peacock feathers are also the identifying symbols of her entourage of *Sylphs* and *Sylphides* (see p. 172).

Zb. król. vol. 801 – k. 079

Vol. II, n. 134

Heroic Female Characters

These two images compare two different versions of heroines: *Armide*, from the ballet *Renaud et Armide* (1758-59) and *Psyche* from the ballet *Psyché et l'Amour* (1762). The two figures have opposing values: the first being "positive" and the second "negative".
The most evident symbols that characterize *Armide* are the sorcerer's wand, the pointed trimming on her overskirt, which is similar to that of the *Demon* (see p. 107), and the symbols of magic inserted into the individual segments of her skirt. The trimming with bows recalls the sensual pleasure with which *Armide* succeeds in capturing *Renaud*; the opulent necklace symbolizes wealth, power and her role as dominator. Her gesture is as elegant and ladylike as it is strong and resolute. And the chromatic play of colors – green, yellow, black and white – is resolute.
Only desperation, however, can express the gesture of the beautiful *Psyche*, who has been condemned by Venus. The figure emanates sweetness and love, both in the drawing and the costume, which is filled with garlands and bows that are interlaced in an asymmetrical manner, conventions that were ascribed to gallant characters. The choice of colors is aimed at creating a precious and, at the same time, delicate effect: a white dress covered in pink highlights (ribbons and bows) and enlivened with the greenery from rose garlands.

Zb. król. vol. 802 – k. 041

Zb. król. vol. 801 – k. 038

Heroic Male Characters

These images from volume VIII (University of Warsaw Library) compare two different male characters: the perfidious *Danaus*, from the ballet *Hypermnestre ou les Danaïdes* (Stuttgart, 1764), and the heroic *Aeneas*, from the ballet *Énée et Didon* (Stuttgart, between 1760 and 1766). The regalness of the former is indicated by his scepter, the imposing crown from which a tall plume issues forth, the broad cape and the sumptuousness of the fabrics, which play on the contrast between dark yellow and purple.
Also regal is the attitude taken by *Aeneas*, whose suit is crowned by a headdress in the shape of a Roman helmet. This constitutes the base of a plume of extraordinary dimensions, which announces the character's elevated rank. The costume plays on symbols in praise of love (the segmented band ending with a gallant bow) and elements from Roman costumes (leather strips on the short skirt and shoulders, the breastplate of fake metal scales). The dominant color, however – sky blue – seems more intended to reflect the ballet's plot, which fundamentally centers on the love between Dido and Aeneas, rather than the latter's departure for Carthage.

Zb. król. vol. 802 – k. 004

Zb. król. vol. 802 – k. 099

Secondary Mythological Figures as Followers of the Divinities

The secondary mythological figures that populated numerous ballets were equally characterized by soft curves and captivating asymmetry. As documentation for this type of character, we have selected a *Faun* from the tenth volume in Warsaw and a *Bacchante* from the ballet *La Descente d'Orphée aux Enfers*, which is in the seventh volume of the same collection (but reproduced here from the collection in Stockholm).

The identifying elements in both sketches here are numerous, and they relate to both costume and gesture. To begin with the costumes, each sketch features an ochre-colored wild fur over-garment covered with dark spots. Here, the furs, although an essential symbolic element, actually appear to function as a pretext for the refined and gallant decorations. Also gallant is the sinuous, bowed trimming on the *tonnelet* worn by the *Faun*, whose half-uncovered chest, left so by a garment with a marked oblique cut, is an acknowledgment of the iconography for fauns, which, as we have seen on page 51, had already been institutionalized some forty years previously. As Noverre considered necessary to specify, the effect of nudity, fundamental for this type of character (see also the *Gladiateurs*, p. 120), was rendered through tight-fitting, flesh-colored fabrics.

The *Bacchante*'s decorative ivy leaves and tambourines are, on the other hand, a clear evocation of classical iconography, in which ivy and the thyrsus were used to identify the god Bacchus and the feasts held in his honor (bacchanalia). The figure's broad gesture gives the impression of an airy and dynamic dance, well-matched to the character of a follower of Bacchus or an interpreter of the bacchanalia.

Zb. król. vol. 804 – k. 74

Vol. II, n. 98

Fantastical Characters

These images from volume X of the collection at the University of Warsaw document Noverre's conception of the fantastical character – in this case, a male *Sylph* and a *Triton*. The richly-decorated suits and high, feather-laden headdresses, as well as the conventional, representative fashioning of the costumes, all connect these figures to the retinue of one of the divinities, which explains why Noverre would categorize them in the *sérieux* genre.

The *Sylph*, in keeping with classical tradition, is understood to be a follower of Juno, who appears in the guise of *Iuno Cœlestis*, Goddess of the Heavens (see p. 100); and the selection of ornamentation – sparse clouds on the garment and bodice, and an abundance of feathers from a peacock, the bird sacred to the goddess – derives from this. The height of the plumes on the *Sylph*'s head and the roundness of his short skirt, which appears like a *tonnelet* of reduced dimensions, underline the character's official role as a follower of Juno, queen of the heavens, which requires of him an elegance and good taste worthy of a member of a royal court and an adherence to the latest fashion trends (note the asymmetry of the decorations).

Also in his depiction of the *Triton*, Boquet wanted to emphasize the character's role as a follower of a divinity – in this case, of Neptune: the headdress is important and erect, and the ornaments (starfish, seaweed, coral, etc.) are positioned in a very organized manner, forming a particularly elegant entirety suitable for a member of the court. The conventional workmanship in the *Triton*'s costume signals the influence of academic ballet from the Paris Opera, with its own specific fashions.

Zb. król. vol. 804 – k. 05

Zb. król. vol. 804 – k. 040

Allegories

Following 18th-Century tradition, Noverre frequently resorted to the use of allegoric figures. These include various characters, depending on the context and on the function assigned to them in the choreographic and dramatic structure of the ballet. Two characters have been selected for this brief sampling below, both designated as "positive": the allegory of *Games and Laughter* and that of the *Pleasures*. Both figures were drawn for the ballet *Psyché* and were inserted by Noverre into the seventh of the eleven volumes presented to Stanislaw II August of Poland in 1766.
From the ballet's plot, one can deduce the fundamental roles of these characters in this scene: dancing and characterization; and this explains why they always appear as a male/female couple.
The costumes are extremely conventional, and, as with those of the *Bergers* and *Bergères*, they conform to fashion styles at the Paris Opera. Bows and garlands are abundant, while the trimmings and crossings of ribbons create soft, sinuous curves that summon up charm, joy and also a veiled sensuality.
The plumes on these male costumes, high and majestic, stand out against the ladies' headwear, which, as we see below, right, and also on previous pages, is contained and quite refined.

Zb. król. vol. 801 – k. 045

Zb. król. vol. 801 – k. 048

Passions Personified

The need to confer dramatic weight to extreme situations induced Noverre to utilize "personification", an instrument borrowed from French lyric theater. These images gather together the costume sketches for *Desperation* and *Vengeance* (from *Renaud et Armide*, 1758-59), which form part of volume VIII of the collection in Warsaw. All of the costumes confer upon the figures a frightening aspect that lends itself to the *grotesque* genre, which is further exaggerated, as Noverre states, by the fact that they were interpreted by male performers.
Their faces are covered by terrifying masks with mouths opened frighteningly. Daggers, flames and serpents – on the arms, in the hands and wrapped around the bodies – indicate the wickedness and destructive impulses that animate the soul of Armide the sorceress, abandoned by Renaud. In many cases, such characters would also have had a Gorgon's head reproduced on their garments, belts or other parts of the costume. *Vengeance* (right) is dressed in tongues of flame.
Clear signs of a "negative" character are the broken lines and lively angles that predominate in the clothing, creating jagged and zigzagged edges. This concept is inherited from traditional iconography, which attributes a negative value to angles and pointed shapes, in clear contrast to the curved lines visible in the "positive" character's costume (see also p. 59, bottom).
It is no coincidence that in this same era, theoreticians and the lettered – like Edmund Burke and Voltaire, for example – would identify the quality of softness and the curved line with the sensitive attribute of "grace". As Carlo Blasis demonstrates in his *Traité élémentaire théorique et pratique de l'Art de la danse* (Milan, 1820), this concept was to remain in academic dance as a basic aesthetic principle. Drawing on Burke, Blasis insistently recommends the avoidance of angles and broken lines, inasmuch as these are not only technically flawed, but also "*grotesques*".

Zb. król. vol. 802 – k. 061

Zb. król. vol. 802 – k. 059

Evil Figures

These characters from the ballet *Psyché* – the *Demon* and the *Fates* – from volume VII of the collection in Warsaw, are placed together here to underscore the highly "negative" role afforded to angularity and acute shapes, and to accent the depersonalizing and emblematic function of the *Demon*'s mask.

Zb. król. vol. 801 – k. 053

Zb. król. vol. 801 – k. 050

Zb. król. vol. 804 – k. 077

For the character *Folly*, which was to remain unaltered until the 1780s, Noverre and Boquet stayed faithful to iconographic tradition. The maiden is holding a "marotte" (jester's stick), and her dress has zigzags and contrasting chromatics, conventional symbols of the non-linear, or irrational, behavior of the follies.

"National" Characters

In 18th-Century terminology, a ballet was defined as "national" when the setting was entirely of one country and, in addition to the customs, the fundamental traits of the clothing also referred to the same.
On this page, we bring together figures from the *"camp" Ballet Hongrois*, composed by Noverre during his period in Stuttgart (1760-1766). The movements are all strongly characterized, as are the costumes, with an explicit declaration of "national style". These sketches appear in both the collection in Warsaw (1766, vol. IX) and that in Stockholm (1791, vol. II).

Vol. II, n. 17

Vol. II, n. 16

Vol. II, n. 18

Vol. II, n. 20

Comparing these sketches of the *Janissaire* (a Turkish soldier) and *Icoglan* (a page) from *Les Jalousies ou les Fêtes du Sérail* (1758) with the drawing below, from the collection of traditional costumes published as a series by Braun & Schneider between 1861 and 1880, one can see the application of the principle of verisimilitude. As in the costume of the *Chinoise* (see p. 92), the traditional costume, though revisited in theatrical form and embellished with luxurious ornamentation, remains true to the essential features of the original.

Vol. II, n. 7 — Vol. II, n. 10

Türkisches Militär (Janitscharen).

The *Eunuch* and the *Janissary* (personal guard of the Turkish sultan) demonstrate the style that saturates the ballet *Les Jalousies ou les Fêtes du Sérail*. The ballet was created by Noverre in 1758, immediately after the abolition of the mask.

Vol. II, n. 5

Vol. II, n. 6

Vol. II, n. 14

This *Peruvian* shows us how the distant Americas were seen in the European imagination during the 1700s. Elements gathered from traditional costumes are blended together with features typical of theater costumes to create a spectacular totality.

Between Frivolous Games and Rococo Charm: *Les Petits riens* by Noverre and Mozart

On June 11, 1778 – after a performance of the opera *Le Finte Gemelle* by Niccolò Piccinni – a ballet by Noverre that had already been produced in Vienna ten years earlier took to the stage of the Paris Opera: *Les Petits riens*. While retaining the original music, the ballet also presented new musical numbers composed specifically for the occasion by Mozart.
In this new version, the ballet consisted of three distinct scenes, presented separately as in *opéra-ballet*, but connected by a thread of playful games. Noverre had wanted to offer his Parisian public a joyous, frivolous ballet in the Rococo style still fashionable in the French capital.

In the first scene, *Cupid* is captured and imprisoned. The second scene takes the game of Blind Man's Bluff as inspiration, while in the third scene, two shepherdesses fall in love with a shepherd, who is in fact another shepherdess in disguise. Performing the first scene were Marie-Madeleine Guimard and the barely eighteen-year-old Auguste Vestris; the main character of the second scene was taken by Dauberval, while the third little scene was interpreted by Paris Opera stars Marie-Madeleine Guimard, Marie Allard and Mademoiselle Asselin (as the masquerading shepherd).
That the inspiration came from painting is more than evident, as the game of Blind Man's Bluff had been painted by artists of the caliber of Jean-Honoré Fragonard, while the capture of *Cupid* was indeed a favorite theme for painters and decorators. The costumes designed for the occasion brought out the gallant and fashionable qualities that Noverre wanted to impress upon the ballet, but at the same time, they display an adaptation of the traditional schemes. An accentuated geometry in the structure and decorations is noticeable in both costumes.
The youth (top) wears a red *tonnelet* with light-colored embroidery. The maiden's costume is a play of contrast between red, white and blue, and has a homogenous and symmetrical structure that is in strident contrast to the "beautiful disorder" of the costumes that Boquet had designed in Stuttgart.

This painting by Fragonard, entitled *Blind Man's Bluff* (1760), is extremely representative of the frivolous tones and sensuality that characterize Rococo and late-Rococo painting. Fragonard was a friend of the celebrated Paris Opera danseuse Marie-Madeleine Guimard, who, in turn, was closely connected through friendship to Dauberval. The brio, vivacity of gesture and lightness (of fabrics and color) that characterize this painting are clear signs of a shared taste that surely had its equivalent in the dance of the *Pâtres Galants* (Gallant Shepherds). It is therefore no accident that the subject would have offered Noverre inspiration for the second scene of his ballet, *Les Petits riens*.

The 1761 painting by François Boucher (*Portrait of Madame Baudouin*) and the group of porcelain figures from Meissen, which dates back to 1741, both bear witness to the popularity of the caged bird theme. The reason for this was its dualistic meaning: a bird inside or outside the cage symbolized, respectively, the preservation or loss of virginity.

Here below are two neoclassical versions of the love-bird in a cage, demonstrating the wide diffusion of this theme. The interpretation of the bird as a little Cupid, who is either captured in a net or sold from a basket, was inspired by the large fresco uncovered at Herculaneum, *The Market of Love*, reproduced here below (right) in a 1763 interpretation by Joseph-Marie Vien, entitled *The Cupid Seller* (Musée National du Château, Fontainebleau).

Neoclassical Interpretations in Costumes from Noverre's Ballets

The images presented on the following pages have been selected to highlight different versions of the same characters, designed by Louis-René Boquet some twenty to thirty years apart.

The differences, at times substantial, place in relief the effect on Boquet of changes in taste that affected all of the arts between the 1770s and 1780s, and the influence of emerging Neoclassicism. The dependence on fashion and Rococo taste already appears to have been greatly reappraised: the *tonnelets* have disappeared completely, and a further reduction has occurred in the width of women's dresses, which now seem to have acquired a rounded form. Also abandoned are the white wigs, with women's hairstyles now showing their natural hair colors.

The symbology peculiar to Baroque theater, inspired by traditional classical iconography, is much less apparent, limited to evocative signs attached to certain parts of the clothing (note especially the details in *Medée et Armide* on p. 116). The gestures have lost the rigidity and conventionality that had characterized the drawings from the early 1760s, and they have acquired a notable expressive intensity. Various costume sketches show accentuated expression in the fingers, which were considered by the English actor David Garrick (and thus by Noverre) as "speaking tongues".

The figures to follow are sources valuable in comprehending the changes in taste that regarded both the costume in general and the presentation of characters.

Vol. II, n. 39

Vol. II, n. 51

Vol. II, n. 47

Horace, from the ballet *Les Horaces et les Curiaces* (1774), is quite similar in both costume and gesture to *Pyrrhus*, from the ballet *Pyrrhus et Polyxène* (1760-1766), but missing is the conventional, affected tone of the Rococo model: the typical gallant bow is absent, and the gesture has gained a new intensity. The same transformation can be seen in the *Gladiateurs* (see p. 120), in relation to the analogous *Lutteurs* of the early 1760s, inasmuch as the clothing and gestures have become both essential and vigorous.

Zb. król. vol. 802 – k. 004

1766

Vol. II, n. 42

1791

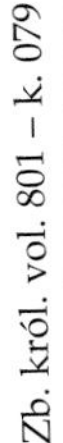

Zb. król. vol. 801 – k. 079

1766

Vol. II, n. 109

1791

These examples of female characters assist in our quest to understand how the character of the sorceress was transformed. The broken lines and sharp angles (indicators of evil) have disappeared by 1791, while the symbols of magic have been transformed into elegant decorations. In 1791, *Armide* is also presented without a wand.

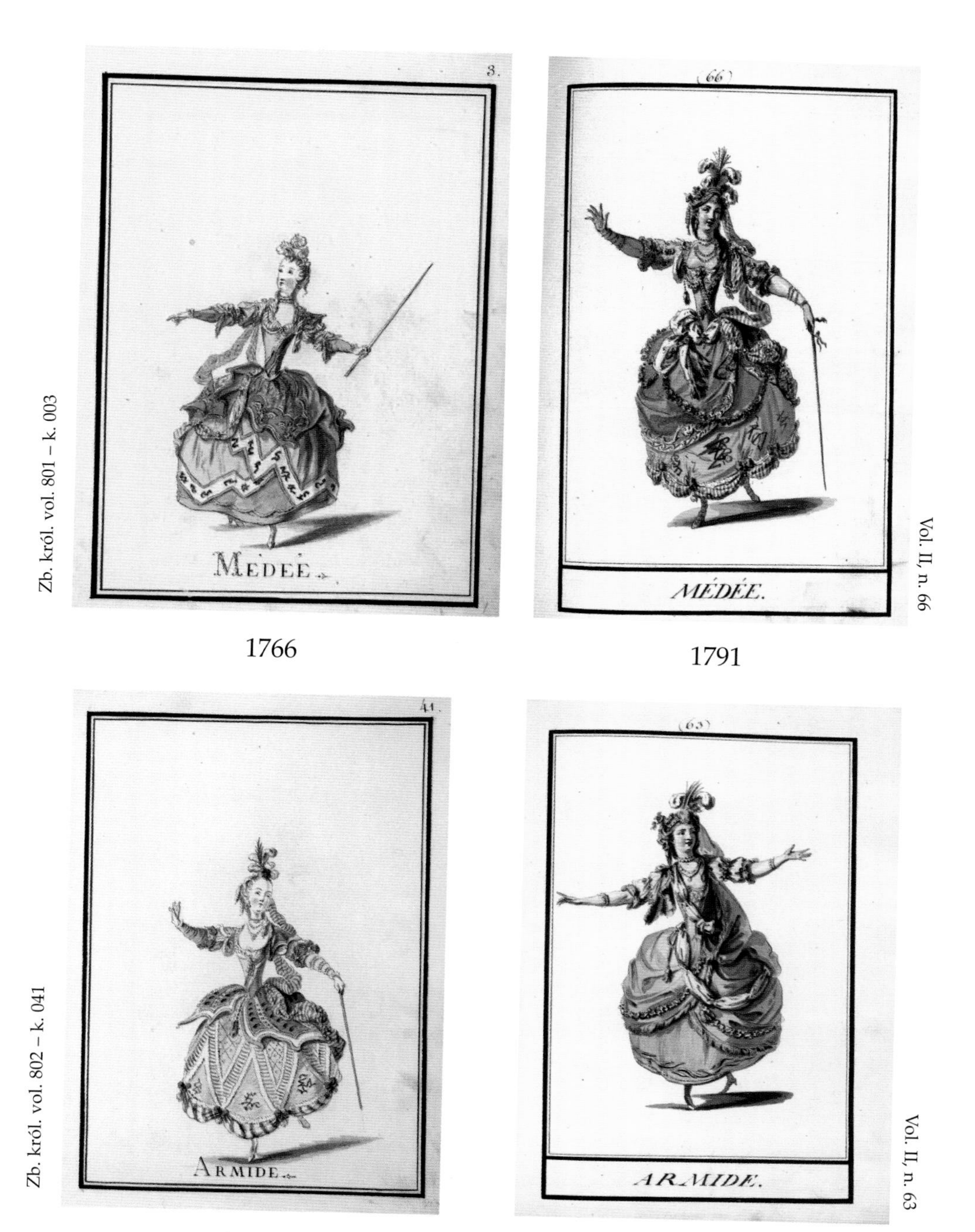

Zb. król. vol. 801 – k. 003

1766

Vol. II, n. 66

1791

Zb. król. vol. 802 – k. 041

Vol. II, n. 63

1766

1791

Psyche's bows and small roses have been discarded. *Happy Shadow* ("the youthful lover expired") from the ballet *La Descente d'Orphée aux Enfers* (The Descent of Orpheus to the Underworld), who was previously heavily decorated with bows, has been transformed into a mysterious figure, with her face covered by a veil.

Zb. król. vol. 801 – k. 038

1766

Vol. II, n. 113

1791

Zb. król. vol. 801 – k. 074

1766

Vol. II, n. 56

1791

By 1791, the savage aspect of *Iarbes* (from *Énée et Didon*) has been abandoned, and he wears a costume that Boquet had created in the 1760s for an African figure that appears in volume XI of the collection in Warsaw. The *Triton* is not dressed as a member of Neptune's court, but is marked by a meaningful realism in both gesture and costume.

Zb. król. vol. 801 – k. 101

Vol. II, n. 68

1766

1791

Zb. król. vol. 804 – k. 038

Vol. II, n. 89

1766

1791

The Perpetuation of Iconographic Tradition

While the differences between the 1766 and 1791 versions, highlighted on the preceding pages, are substantial, the same cannot be said for some of the character typologies: the *Personifications*, the *Allegories* and certain divinities, whose presence in ballet is symbolic and whose attributes are dictated by conventions that would still be respected. Of note in the figure of *Apollo*, nevertheless, are the transformation of the buckled shoes into Greek-style sandals and the elimination of the elegant puffed sleeves.

Zb. król. vol. 802 – k. 026

1766

Vol. II, n. 124

1791

Zb. król. vol. 801 – k. 049

1766

Vol. II, n. 146

1791

Costume sketch by Louis-René Boquet for the *Gladiateurs*, 1780s; vol. II, no. 34, National Library of Sweden. The "nude" effect, as we have seen on page 103, was realized with tight-fitting, flesh-colored fabric.

From Mythology to Everyday Life at the End of the *Ancien Régime*

Dance at the Paris Opera in the 1760s and -70s

Extravagance and Luxury at the Opéra

In the traditionally-molded academic ballets at the Paris Opera, the lack of expressive characterization for dancers and the presence of masks (which would be abandoned definitively at the beginning of the 1770s) inspired both a strengthening of technique and an exaggeration in costuming, as these were the only instruments available to affirm the value of dance. Fashion often served as the primary source of inspiration. In the drawing above by Louis-René Boquet (ca. 1757), the influence of fashion is expressed in the *rocaille* (shell motif), which is typical of Rococo, and in the extraordinary width of the garments.

The **Pâtre** *Style*

The evolution of the style of *pas de pâtre* (shepherd's step) during the 1770s is demonstrated in two famous engravings from 1779 that portray Dauberval – a follower of Noverre, as we have seen, since 1757 – together with Marie-Madeleine Guimard and Marie Allard in a lively *pas de trois*.
Observing the engraving below, one recognizes – in the wide, confident movements of their bodies, and in the play of the arms that has them linking together – the influence exerted by the *Allemande* dance (see next page). But in the dynamism of the movements – which does not run counter to the academic elegance of the gestures – the importance attained by the *comique* genre during the era of Louis XVI is evident. Driven by the dance and by a sense of veiled complicity, their bodies shift away from verticality, or *aplomb*, assuming various positions.
In the confidence of the poses and the expressiveness of the movements, which appear to translate a conversation into dance, one cannot help but notice the signs of the process of assimilation between technique and pantomime that was set in motion between the 1770s and -80s, aided by the aesthetic line that was affirmed during Louis XVI's reign.

The Raising of the Arms

These images from the book *Caractères de la danse Allemande* by the French master Guillaume (Paris, ca. 1769) show the diverse exchanges and interlacing of arms of a couple whose attire declares them to be members of the bourgeoisie. The raising of the arms and displacement of the hands above the head are, by now, common in social dances of the aristocracy and upper bourgeoisie, as well as in those of the lower social classes.
In the figures below, note the presence of the apron, an integral element in the traditional costume.

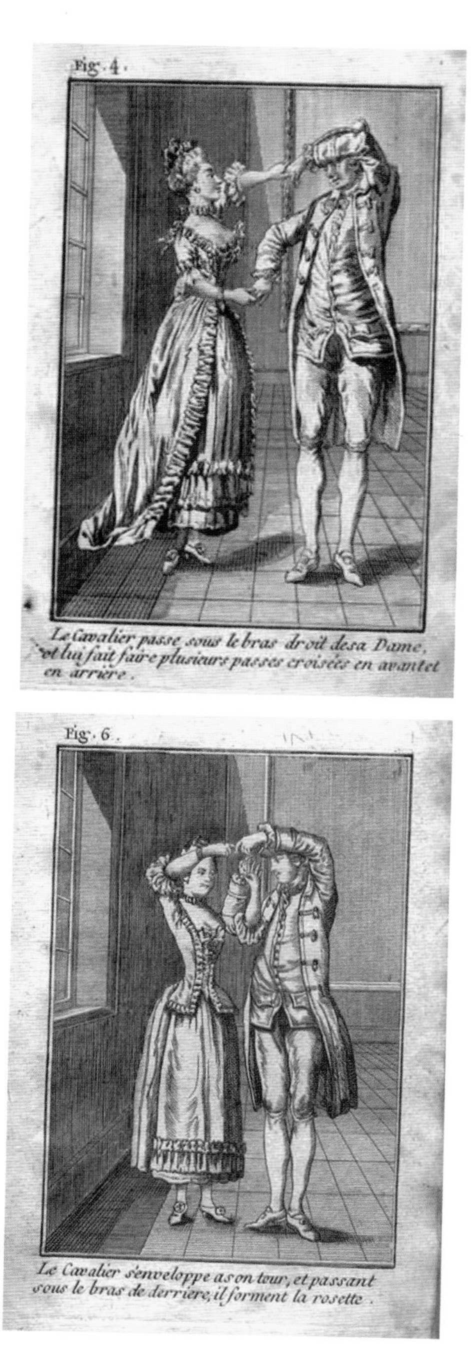

The Stylization of National Dances

These porcelain figurines from the factory in Ludwigsburg (designed by Joseph Ness, 1765; right) and those below, from the Porcelain Museum at the Residenzschloss in Ludwigsburg, show the crossing of arms in dances of Venetian influence. As one can see, the gestures are standardized, and the movements appear generally free of all coarseness. The hairstyles and clothes, although retracing the traditional costume, are styled and embellished with refined decorations. Also in this case, the apron is an integral part of the costume, representing a characteristic element of the traditional costume.

We witness here a process of stylistic adaptation comparable to that which led to the flourishing of theatrical versions of national dances, which were packed into the French and, above all, Italian ballets during the second half of the 18th Century.

The Last Queen of France and Her Love of Dance

The arts and music education given to Marie Antoinette was both accurate and intense, thanks to the guidance of her teachers, Pietro Metastasio and Christoph Willibald Gluck. She studied dance with Noverre from 1767, when she was twelve, until her departure for Paris in 1770, as bride to the future King Louis XVI. Noverre had been engaged by her mother, the Austrian Empress Maria Theresa, as *maître de ballets* of the imperial theaters and director of the performances given at court, In Vienna, as during her sojourn in France, Marie Antoinette loved to perform in ballets presented at the court.

This 1765 painting by J. G. Weikert (right) shows *Le Triomphe de l'Amour* by Franz Anton Hilverding, a ballet performed at the palace of Schönbrunn by the Archdukes Ferdinand and Maximilian and the Archduchess Marie Antoinette (who was not yet ten) on the occasion of the second marriage of their brother Joseph II, which took place on January 24, 1765. The positions of Marie Antoinette and her brothers appear correct, both technically and stylistically.

This painting, by the same artist and from the same year, portrays the daughters of Austrian Empress Maria Theresa in *Il Parnaso Confuso* by Gluck (libretto by Metastasio), performed at the same 1765 event. Through their attitudes and placement, we can see that this is a pantomime scene, executed with the manners and composure expected of the members of a royal family, but with a theatricality and command of the performance space worthy of professional dancers.

Industrious Villages and Merry Peasants: the Paris Opera on the Threshold of the Revolution

With the beginning of Louis XVI's reign, the aesthetic changes in French dance already manifested in the early 1770s were to become yet more evident, above all at the Paris Opera, where general changes in taste and new artistic trends were reflected.
The influences were varied, complex and of diverse origins (and among these, the tastes and preferences of the young French queen are not to be underestimated). After the 1775 Paris Opera production of Gluck's *La Cythère assiégée* (The Siege of Cythera), which had been inspired the homonymous 1748 *opéra-comique* by Charles-Simon Favart, ballet titles inspired by well-known *opéras-comiques* by Favart or by Jean-François Marmontel's moral tales began to appear with growing frequency on the opera playbills.
The French scene was no longer to be dominated by themes garnered from antiquity, but would instead gather together worthy stories set in villages and farming contexts. These were to cheer the public not only through the interpreters' decorous attitudes, but also with stunts and jokes, and minor trickery performed by shrewd maidens.

This was a movement true and proper that, between new productions and revivals, covered a rather substantial period of time, extending into the early 19^{h} Century; and it concerned all of the major exponents of French dance, including Maximilien Gardel, Noverre and Dauberval. Among the most highly acclaimed of the ballets in this genre were Gardel's *La Chercheuse d'esprit* and *Ninette à la cour* (Paris Opera, 1778), and Dauberval's *La Fille mal gardée* (Bordeaux, 1789), a ballet that would be reworked by Paolo Taglioni in 1864 and later created anew by Frederick Ashton in 1960.
The Grape Harvester, by Jean-Honoré Fragonard (1748-52, Fowler McCormick Collection, Chicago): delightful evidence from the 1750s, useful in comprehending the refined reading of popular subjects in ballets from the era of Louis XVI.

This early 19th-Century engraving by Prud'hon, after a drawing by Sébastien Coeuré, portrays Marie-Madeleine Guimard in the role of *Nicette* in *La Chercheuse d'esprit* (The Spirit-Searcher), a ballet staged by Maximilien Gardel at the Paris Opera in 1778. The theme was inspired by the *opéra-comique* of the same title by Charles-Simon Favart, which had been performed at the Opéra-Comique theater in 1741.
Induced by her mother to marry a wealthy old man, *Nicette* manages to get him to enter into a "more proper" marriage with her own mother.
The courteous yet frivolous attitude taken by Guimard in the role of *Nicette* is enhanced by her costume, which, although slightly retouched in the early 19th Century, remains highly expressive. The bodice with crossed laces in front, the bonnet decorated with flowers, the apron and the charming puffed sleeves all place her in a rural setting. But this is in fact simply a polite and elegant stylization of a traditional costume, inspired by women's fashions, as is the maiden's gesture – a delectable interpretation of Rococo taste in this character by Favart.

We have come a long way since that momentous year 1753, when Madame Favart had appeared in the comedy *Bastien et Bastienne*, also by Favart, dressed in an innovatively realistic costume.
This terracotta *Chercheuse d'esprit* by Claude-François Attiret (ca. 1774, Musée des Beaux-Arts, Dijon) is one of the many objects that bear witness to the favor enjoyed by Favart's *opéras-comiques* during the 1770s.
Compared to the refinement and elegance of the dancer Guimard, the simplicity and realism in Attiret's terracotta underlines how the *gracieux-galant* style that had been so representative of French ballet during the first half of the 18th Century was still in vogue at the Paris Opera, above all, in the *demi-caractère* genre.

Men's Costumes Simplified in the **Comique-Pâtre** *Genre*

The aesthetic line affirmed at the Paris Opera during the late 1770s is given further interesting testimony in this *pas de trois* (trio), performed in 1779 by Dauberval, Marie-Madeleine Guimard and Marie Allard (and already discussed on page 123). The man's costume has been much simplified, reduced to plain breeches and a shirt, with a broad sash at the waist. Gone are the precious decorations typical of the preceding period; and the ladies' costumes are also more linear and have been updated to current fashions. Rather eye-catching, on the other hand, is the lively and flamboyant garland, a symbol of joyousness, but also of gallantry and love.

Here to the left is a portrait of one of the two female performers of this trio: Marie-Madeleine Guimard, star of the Paris Opera during the late 1780s. The portrait (entitled *Marie-Madeleine Guimard*) was painted around 1769 by Jean-Honoré Fragonard, friend of the famous ballerina. The painting is in the collection of the Musée du Louvre / A. Dequier – M. Bard in Paris.

The Influence of New Genre Painting

The themes of these two paintings (pp. 130 and 131) are further testimony as to just how much French ballet shared certain tendencies and subjects with the worlds of literature and visual arts.

Dauberval himself was happy to refer to the influence on his creative veins of Pierre-Antoine Baudouin's painting *Une jeune fille querellée par sa mère* (1764). The ballet referred to by Dauberval was his *Le Ballet de la Paille, ou Il n'est qu'un pas du mal au bien* (The Ballet of the Straw, or There is Only One Step from Bad to Good, Grand Théâtre de Bordeaux, July 1, 1789), whose spiritedly moralizing title would be modified two years later to become *La Fille mal gardée* (or The Wayward Daughter). On the left of the painting, a youth is seen escaping up the stairs, a clear sign of the girl's "guilt", which will allow *Lise* (in Dauberval's ballet) to avoid marriage with the foolish *Alain*, and thus to crown her dream of love by instead marrying the one she loves.

Here is a portrait of Dauberval's wife, Madame Théodore (left), in the role of *Lise* from the ballet *La Fille mal gardée*. The coiffure, the dress and the pail at the end of a stick are all reminiscent of the well-mannered realism in Charles-Simon Favart's *opéras-comiques*.

This painting by Étienne Aubry, *La Bergère des Alpes* (1775, Detroit Institute of Arts), documents the favor enjoyed by the homonymous "moral tale" by Jean-François Marmontel, which dates back to 1759. The theme, already used in 1763 by the painter Claude-Joseph Vernet and by the Czech composer Josef Kohaut in a pastorale (Paris, 1766), was then translated by Noverre into a ballet in 1794, entitled *Adelaïde ou la Bergère des Alpes*.

Architecture arabesque d'Herculanum, table number 19 from volume II of the book by the abbot Richard de Saint-Non entitled *Voyage pittoresque ou description des Royaumes de Naples et de Sicile* (1781-86). This drawing by Paris (engraved by Bertheauld) testifies to the deep meaning given to the expression *arabesque* in France at the end of the 18th Century. The architecture described as *arabesque* is imaginary and has great decorative value.

The *Arabesque*: Emblem of "Modern" Dance

The Pictorial *Arabesque*

It is quite impossible to introduce even a brief discussion of the choreographic *arabesque* without first emphasizing how different and unrelated the meaning of the 18th-Century pictorial *arabesque* was from that of Arabic figurative culture.
In the 1700s, the pictorial *arabesque* was synonymous with the Italian *grottesca* (grotesque), a term indicating that peculiar decorative style invented by Raphael and inspired by the frescoes discovered in Rome at the Domus Aurea (in the early 16th Century). Various documents testify to the interchangeability between the two terms *grotesque* and *arabesque* in the 18th Century. The most authoritative and well-known among these are the articles by Claude-Henri Watelet (*Grotesques*) and Louis de Jaucourt (*Peinture*), published in Diderot and d'Alembert's *Encyclopédie* in 1757 and 1765, respectively. Equally important are the various engraved reproductions of the frescoes at Herculaneum contained in *Le Antichità di Ercolano,* a publication released by the Regia Stamperia in Naples between 1755 and 1792, and in the work written by the abbot Saint-Non, entitled *Voyage pittoresque ou Description des Royaumes de Naples et de Sicile*, which was published in Paris between 1781 and 1786.
The articles in the *Encyclopédie*, in particular, not only underscore the analogy between the finds at Nero's Domus Aurea and those from the digs at Herculaneum and Pompeii (which began in 1738 and 1748, respectively), but they also make clear that the new expression *arabesque* was more in keeping with *grotesque*, the root word of which – grotto – refers to the condition of the antique Roman residences before they were 'liberated' from the accumulation of earth under which they had been buried for centuries.
These two fragments of wall painting from a villa at Herculaneum, reproduced on page 132 of the above-mentioned book by Saint-Non and also here below, were described as "Arabesques". They not only constitute unequivocal documentation of the meaning attributed to *arabesque* during the 1700s, but they also reveal how the expression implied the imaginary-fantastic component of this ancient pictorial style, which had fascinated Europe between the 16th and 18th Centuries so much as to become a true and proper fashion during the period of the French Revolution.

Creativity and Extravagance in the "Grotesque-Arabesque"

Peculiarities of the ancient decorative style imitated first by Raphael in the early 1500s, and then, during the 1700s, by the decorators of aristocratic residences include the bizarreness of the approach, and the proportions and shapes – clear signs of the *grotesque*'s detachment from classical rules on the idealized imitation of nature.

In this fragment of decoration by Raphael, from a pillar at the Vatican's Logge (1517-19), lamps, floral motifs and a half-human, half-plant face are all mixed together with neither a nexus, nor any respect for proportion. The figures float in a space stripped of depth, released from the forces of gravity, due to their belonging to a world of fantasy.

This fresco from the early 1700s, at Villa Mansi on the outskirts of Lucca, Italy, demonstrates how French-style lightness and elegance could transform monstrous chimeras into refined and fascinating fantasy creatures. This representative mode was to be well-received in the choreographic world, allowing space for those characters which, having been created outside the canons or in contradiction to the laws on the imitation of human movement, would initially be labeled as *attitude-arabesque*, then simply *arabesque*.

The Choreographic *Arabesque*

The term *arabesque* was to merge into the vocabulary of the terpsichorean arts during the last decade of the 18th Century, riding the incoming wave of Greek-style fashion. There was no precise and unified meaning connected to it, but in all the various ways in which it appeared, the expression revealed clear signs of being conditioned by the trends in taste and, in particular, by the fashion for decorating the salons of residences for the wealthy with imitations of the ancient *bas-reliefs*. Thus, the earliest definition attributed to the choreographic *arabesque,* at the end of the 18th Century, was one of figurative composition in the style of antiquity, imitative of the dances, processions and bacchanalia recovered from archaeological sites or produced in the late 1700s and based on ancient models.

This fresco on a mythological theme, from the Hotel de la rue de la Victoire in Paris and now preserved at the Malmaison, shows the predilection to represent dances and bacchanalia that was widespread among decorators and their clients at the end of the 1700s. The figures are all positioned on the same level, and they are linked in a way similar to that which would be used in choreography.

This fresco from Herculaneum (below), reproduced in the late 18th-Century album *Peintures d'Herculanum,* which is preserved at the Louvre, revisits evocative moments in the music and dance of ancient Rome. In this case, as in other scenes, figures frequently appear with their back turned toward the observer. The angled position "à dos tourné" (with the back turned) would be – as is evident on pages 141, 157 and 158 – one of the innovations produced by choreographers between the end of the 18th Century and the early 19th Century; and it is one of the distinctive traits of the *arabesques*.

The *Arabesque*: Between Eccentricity and Ideal Beauty

Alongside the first definition of *arabesque* in dance indicating a stylish choreographic arrangement that imitated the *bas-reliefs* and friezes of ancient art, another interpretation quickly took shape. And this was more profound and indeed closer to that extravagance and caprice – that "delirium of painting" – with which the pictorial *arabesque-grotesque* would be identified during the decade of the French Revolution. The idealized imitation of nature, founding principle of all the imitative arts, had been the trigger for the process of systemization realized by the Académie Royale de Danse during the era of Louis XIV. In dance technique, this idealized imitation of nature implied the observation of body shape and respect for the natural laws of movement. These elements had generated the technical principles of *en dehors* and *aplomb* and the rules for opposition between the legs and arms, as well as their asymmetric arrangement (see pp. 24-25 and 29).
Why, asked dancers such as Auguste Vestris, deny to oneself the possibility of rivaling the beauty of classical art? Why refuse that Dionysian and unconventional aspect of the ancient arts that had been returned to culture through the digs at Herculaneum and Pompeii, or ignore the fascinating *arabesque*-decorations that, thanks to printed reproductions, were invading the designs for furnishings, table objects and jewels? Thus, it was with an understanding of the *arabesque* as embodying bizarreness and a creative liberty inspired by ancient art that the new generation of choreographers afforded legitimacy to the new positions that had neither *aplomb*, nor opposition between the legs and arms, and to positions with the arms and hands extended into the air – like the *Winged Victory* of Roman art – as light as the danseuses from Herculaneum.

Apollonian and Dionysian Aspects in Ancient Art

These images from the album *Peintures d'Herculanum* (late 18th Century), conserved at the Louvre in Paris, present two contrasting aspects of ancient art: Apollonian and Dionysian.
The *Dancing Maenad* below, after the original fresco from the so-called "Villa of Cicero" in Pompeii, is suspended in a void, as if not belonging to the material world. Her positioning, which summons up composure, harmony and grace, with elegant contrasts between the various parts of the body, is like a hymn to the purity of classical art.

The image of the *Centaur*, ridden savagely by the *Maenad*, who has captured and subjugated him, expresses the darker, more morbid side of human nature with great intensity. Both figures display an accentuation and an unseemliness that, in dance, were considered to be the negation of "good taste". It was, however, precisely these splendid Bacchic figures – so ennobled in ancient art – that allowed the transgression known as the *arabesque* into the world of dance.

Veils and Garlands in Arabesque *Compositions*

The lack of depth-of-field that characterizes the decorations and *bas-reliefs* fashionable during the 1790s would be taken up again by Canova in his *bas-reliefs* and Pompeii-style tempera paintings produced at the close of the 18th Century. This composition from 1797-98, reproduced as a print in 1810-12, shows the linking of bodies, crowns of flowers or laurel, and the fluttering veils that were typical of choreographic works of this period and the early 19th Century.

Although produced much later, the choreographic composition below, from English ballet master E. A. Théleur's *Letters on Dancing*, published in 1831, shows figures dressed in Greek style and linked together by veils and garlands, so as to create a single composite and harmonious group. In addition to demonstrating the affinity between dancing and painting, it also testifies to the survival in choreography of Greek-style fashions well into the 1800s.
At the center is *Mercury*; at the right, *Cupid*, recognizable by the quiver and bird's wings, and *Zephyr*, with butterfly wings. On the left: *Psyche*, with wings, and *Flora*.

Noverre's Condemnation of the **Arabesque**

The choreographic *arabesque* corresponds to one of the most significant moments as regards the influence on dance of Greek style, and it remains the most important result of the revolution realized by the new generation of dancers and choreographers. Yet the academic world and the old generation of masters viewed this transformation as a grave violation of tradition and a disgraceful form of degeneration.
In his *Lettres sur la Danse, sur les Ballets et les Arts* (1803-1804), in volume IV, letter number VII, on pages 49-50, Noverre expresses himself on the *arabesques* thusly:

> Could not the *funambulists*, the *acrobats* who spin vortically and the *equilibrists* who are the darlings of the Boulevards reclaim all the "tours de force", the great leaps, the *passes-campagne*, the vortical *pirouettes*, and the indecently excessive poses that we have abstracted from them? This new genre has been called *Arabesque*. One understands all too well that the dancers are ignorant of the fact that the genre Arabesque is too fantastical and too bizarre to serve as a model for their art.
> The painters maintain that the Arabesque owes its birth to delirium; and they consider it to be an orphan of art.

But it was, in fact, the official models that had opened the doors to this new form.
Here to the left is a view of the dining room in Pompeian style designed in the late 1700s by Charles Percier for Napoleon and Josephine's Malmaison. Visible between the windows are panels with some of the famous *Hours* by Raphael, as well as those danseuses in the style of Herculaneum, suspended in empty space, that were so condemned by Noverre.

The **Arabesques** *as an Expression of Joy*

About fifteen years later, Carlo Blasis, inheritor of the purest French School, but also aligned with the most modern trends of the "new" school at the Paris Opera, would value the *arabesques'* aspects of originality, elegance and lightness, interpreting the irresolution as the most poetic and fascinating aspect of the new form, saying that "the arabesques are infinite".
The images reprinted below are from Blasis' *Traité élémentaire théorique et pratique de l'Art de la danse*, published in Milan in 1820 and (lower right) from its reissue within *The Code of Terpsichore* (London, 1828). Three of the fourteen plates that illustrate the text present a sampling of the *arabesques* that were most in vogue during the first two decades of the century. Presented here are figures with arms opened and extended outward; positions with both arms gathered softly to one side, as if supporting a lyre; and dynamic positions with the body precariously inclined or with the back forcefully turned to nearly ninety degrees.
All of these, however, emanate that joy with which dance was equated during the neoclassical age. They are characterized by an accentuated dynamism, and they all show that outward radiation in various directions and progressive tapering of lines from the center outward, which, as the theorist on Neoclassicism Francesco Milizia describes in an essay expressly on the "*arabesca*", was typical of the pictorial *arabesque-grotesque* of the 1700s.

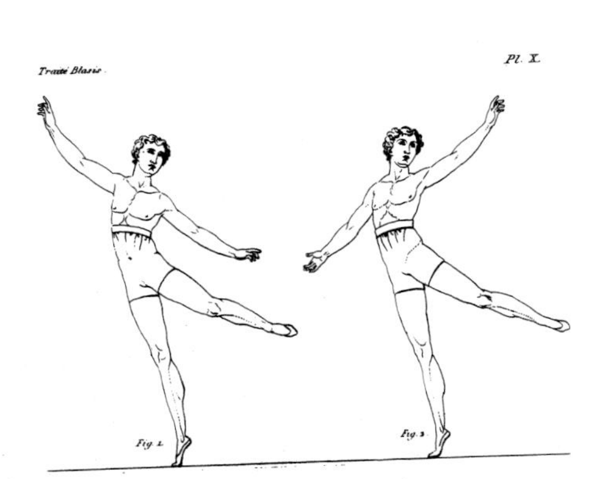

These suggestive images from the *Manuel complet de la danse*, published by Carlo Blasis in Paris in 1830, express with great intensity the transformation of dance in the late 1700s.
The bodies are poised in the air in quite diverse positions, almost as if granting form to the liberty conquered with the affirmation of Neoclassicism and with the social changes at the end of the century. They express the profound importance of the "new" dance, manifesting in their flight that immateriality which would constitute the visible sign of the imaginary and fantastical element of the *arabesque*.
Included in this series of images are also interpretations showing the virtuosic evolution of female dancers, whose bodies are uncovered like the *Winged Victory* of ancient art – weightless figures produced by the imagination, like the future *Sylphides* and *Wilis* of the Romantic ballets.

Innovations Around the Turn of the 19th Century

Cross-Contamination between Dance and Pantomime

From the 1780s onward, and above all during the period of the French Revolution, the world of dance was to be subjected to multiple influences. From salon balls to fashion, from theater to the latest literary currents and most innovative trends in the sphere of figurative arts – all would be transformed when brought together in fertile contact, offering new creative clues and opportunities to the choreographers. The vigor and expressive mobility of the body in national dances and the Italian *grotesque* style flowed back into academic technique. Dramatic theater provided nourishment to pantomime, conceding gestures to it. New social dances, if not yet risen to the heights of aristocratic Olympus, would nevertheless suggest new gestural models. The separation of dance and pantomime, usual in French ballet, was soon to begin to surrender to an ever more recurrent process of assimilation, as regards gestures and steps.

The two images placed together here for comparison are remarkably explicit regarding the confluence of mimed gestures in *la danse proprement dite* (pure dance), or conversely, the transformation of acted gestures into dance movement.

In both the lower image, from *Lezioni di declamazione e d'arte teatrale* by Antonio Morrocchesi, 1832 – with its caption "Gran Dio pietà" (Great God, have mercy) – and the image above, which illustrates Marie-Madeleine Guimard in *Le Premier Navigateur* by Maximilien Gardel (Paris Opera, 1785), the gesture is one of imploring. But the Italian actress' small, composed step forward was to be transformed into a dance step that, a century later, would be called *piqué en arabesque*.

The figure portraying Guimard also constitutes a valuable documentation of the adaptation of the fashionable "informal" style instituted by Marie Antoinette. The very low-heeled slipper fits quite snugly and is fastened at the ankle by "Greek-style" laces. The dress, made of one continuous piece of fabric, is fastened at the waist by a large, colored sash. Her hair is let down and strewn across her back. This ballet, inspired by a poem published in 1763 by Swiss poet Salomon Gessner, carries clear signs of an affirmation of Neoclassicism in ballet at the Paris Opera.

The Universal Language of Pantomime

The most significant example of the transformation of pantomimic gesture into dance is that in which Salvatore Viganò and Maria Medina are portrayed in the *pas de deux pantomime* from the opera *Endymion* by Antonio Muzzarelli, first performed in Vienna in 1793.
These images by Gottfried Schadow (1797; left) and Giuseppe Lancedelli (1793; right) recount a moment representative of amorous skirmish: the youth holds the maiden back, placing his hands on her waist to impede her escape.
Long since gone is the geometric symbolism of the Minuet, in which pursuit and flight were represented by an S-shaped path performed by the interpreters in two opposing directions (see p. 61). Equally far removed is the specular abstraction of the traditional academic ballets that were performed with masks. In *la danse proprement dite* (pure dance), just as in pantomime, male and female roles are distinct, defined by a vocabulary of movements, the function of which relates to the particular situation.

The most characteristic gesture in the *pas de deux* on the preceding page is the forward thrust of the arms, which is accompanied by the body, withdrawn and in flight, with the gaze turned back, as if fleeing from danger.
The origins of this gesture, which Francesco Milizia, in his *Dizionario delle Belle Arti del disegno* (1797), considered to be one of the most important in pantomime, are attributable to Raphael, although its true origins go further back to antiquity. And it is, in fact, present in all of the iconographic repertories – from those of the pictorial and plastic arts to those of the Commedia dell'Arte and Italian dramatic theater – as if Raphael, to whom we owe the first documentation of this gesture, had turned himself into the standard-bearer of a rare and ancient tradition that was deeply rooted in practice.
The following series of images documents some particularly significant cases of the use of this gesture and, at the same time, shows the permeability in this sphere as regards reciprocal influences.

To the right, we see an engraved reproduction from 1578 of Raphael's fresco at the Vatican Logge, *Joseph and Potiphar's Wife* (1517-19). The scheme is clear, and the intention of the gestures in both figures is evident. Joseph's body is inclined forward, thrust toward the same direction as his arms, in an attempt to avoid the provocations of Potiphar's wife. The fearful gaze produces an accentuated turn of the head to the back.

In this engraving by Charles-Alphonse Du Fresnoy (1755) of the marble grouping by Bernini, *Apollo and Daphnis*, the "Raphaelian" scheme, although slightly modified (*Apollo* has already reached *Daphnis*, as she is transformed into a laurel), still preserves the essential mimic elements: the impulse of the arms, the body's almost violent thrust, and the gaze, which is turned toward the impending danger.

The image below, left, documents the presence of gesture in the publication by Antonio Morrocchesi, *Lezioni di declamazione e d'arte teatrale*, which was issued in Florence in 1832. The caption, which reads, "Carlo? Oh, let us escape!" refers unequivocally to a gesture indicating flight.
The same gesture is present in Table 17 of the book *Neue und Curieuse Theatrialische Tantz-Schul* (second part) by Gregorio Lambranzi (Leipzig, 1716), reproduced here below, right; and it is used to express the same intention.

The image here to the left reproduces the *Capricho* number 72 by Goya, which dates back to 1799. Its caption, "No te escaparas" (You will not escape), points unequivocally to flight, but the stylization of the movement and control of the arms bear witness to the process of assimilation into dance of this expressive attitude and its technical development.

These images below attest to the gradual process of assimilation into dance of iconographic schemes and the inevitable move away from their original meaning and toward other expressive intentions.
The top image is from the ballet *Zolova Arfa* by F. Tolstoy (1838); in the figure below: Maria Taglioni in *Giselle* (1841). Note in both images that the dramatic power of the original gesture has given way to a certain poetic tension.

Lady Hamilton's Evocation of the World of Antiquity

Upon arriving in Naples, as a guest of Lord William Hamilton, the British ambassador to Naples, Emma Lyon-Hart became fascinated with the warm atmosphere and floating reminiscence evoked by the wonderful and mysterious world that had just been brought to light through the archaeological excavations: Maenads poetically suspended in void space; audacious representations of Centaurs; and the mute scenes of ancient dramas that were reproduced in the frescoes from the villas at Herculaneum (see pp. 137-138). All these colluded to entice the beautiful English model to create a sort of performance that would evoke the theater of antiquity.

Writing in his diary on December 26, 1786, Lord Hamilton recalls the preparations for Emma's performances. A salon was decorated, first by covering the windows with heavy, dark-blue velvet curtains , blocking out all the light. She had white marble statues and large Greek vases set on marble bases and arranged along the walls. The room was illuminated only by the light from one tall Roman tripod placed in a corner and by small flames set upon the floor. And then Emma appeared, youthful (she was only twenty-one) and very beautiful indeed.

Her tall figure, covered in a white peplos, appeared suddenly in the circle of light, remaining still, while slowly she let her outer veil fall; her sculptured body remained partially covered by her long, tawny hair, gleaming in the light, the locks falling over her breast and loosely over her shoulders and down her back; then she quickly gathered up her hair into a crimson-colored turban wrapped around her head, and with her big eyes, she turned upward to examine the darkness of the skies, while in her hand, she held a plaque, upon which a parchment rested, unrolled and inscribed by the same stylus that she held between her fingers: she was the Cumaean Sybil. Other seductive apparitions of goddesses were to follow, as she wrapped, alternately, either a black or an amaranth-colored shawl over her Greek peplos and assumed, one after the other, the respective aspects of *Circe, Diana the Huntress*, *Cassandra* and *Medea*. And at the end, she violated that cage of flames, and she danced – in bare feet and to a rhythm made by castanets, cymbals and tambourines – the tarantella, revealing the soft, sensual curves of her flexuous hips, her face appearing inebriated, like a Dionysian priestess.

Emma's performances were recounted by poets the likes of Goethe, and she was immortalized in splendid drawings by Francesco Novelli and by the German artist Friedrich Rehberg. Of the eleven *attitudes* drawn by Rehberg and published by Tommaso Piroli in 1794, several are extremely indicative of the coming-of-age of a new movement language. As can be gathered from the images below and on the next page, Emma's body moved from profoundly felt dramatic gestures to a sinuous tambourine dance, of equal expressiveness and vibrancy.
It was an extremely interesting transitional period for dance. And pantomime, as expressive as it was, could not be given credit for the rise of dance as an art form. As Carlo Blasis wrote, dance was art because, with all its various transformations, it had acquired a fresh expressive intensity and vital creative energy.
Emma's *attitudes* spread quickly all around Europe, and they were not only to influence dance at the Opéra, but also to contribute to the diffusion of light, transparent garments and large, wrap-around cashmere shawls. These were the years, in fact, when cashmere (initially imported from Asia) began to be produced in England and France.

Emma Hamilton is portrayed here in the final table (no. XII) of the *attitudes* drawn live by Rehberg and engraved by Tommaso Piroli in 1794. Her gesture is highly dramatic, and her pliant and vibrant body reveals the woman's deeply-felt emotion. The musicality of the composition, the intensity of her body's thrust, the theatricality of her gesture, and the delicacy with which she is portrayed by Rehberg – using the neoclassical technique of "outline drawing" – all conjure up comparison of this *attitude* with the figures from Canova's moving and representative *bas-relief*, *The Death of Priam* (1787-90; below). Both indicate a connection between the body and its emotions, which, when extolled by Blasis, would become the soul of Romantic ballet.

In their research into new forms of equilibrium, dancers of the 18th Century did not hesitate to study the techniques used by acrobats. The various positions of the *Funambulists* from Herculaneum, reproduced here from *Le Antichità di Ercolano,* would also provide a strong stimulus to legitimate the technical development promoted by the new generation.

Innovations in Technique in the Late 18th Century

The opening of new expressive horizons stimulated by Neoclassicism and the affirmation of the right to creative liberties being championed by the new generations of dancers gave free vent to an ostentatious development of technique. The generation of dance artists active at the turn of the century, conditioned by fashion and increasingly receptive culturally, was to hurl itself into experimentation, even recklessly so, never negating, however, the principles of lightness, elegance and formal equilibrium sanctified by the Académie Royale.
The group responsible for these new proposals was diverse, and it included both men and women. In male dance technique, new footwear that fit the foot perfectly allowed the extension of the pointed foot and, consequently, an energetic detachment of the heel away from the floor. This resulted in a general extension of the leg and a greater upward lift of the body. Jumps were to acquire more potency and elevation; *pirouettes* were accelerated; and the number of turns was increased, so much so as to draw comparisons with those of the Dervish monks from Turkey.
Such results were the outcome of concentrated study on the acquisition of balance, stability and resistance, which did not shy away from tackling the practices of Italian acrobats and circus funambulists. Between the condemnations from the academic world and conservative critics, on the one hand, and the provocative examples from Herculaneum – the *Centaurs* and *Funambulists* – on the other, the model of antiquity prevailed in the end; and the *arabesque* was used to give legitimacy to this model, as an expression that held poetic connotations for the younger generation, while for Noverre, it represented his disapproval of "modern" dance (see p. 140).
The way of classifying figures that is seen here in the *Dancing Funambulists*, reproduced on the preceding page from *Le Antichità di Ercolano* (note the Bacchic thyrsus and the musical instruments), offers a very clear indication of the study of poses and positioning that inspired the choreographers at the Paris Opera, and before them, Raphael, for his decoration of the Vatican Logge.
In the assorted figures that squat in different ways, one gathers that this is a systematic study of the various combinations of the arms, legs, torso and gaze. The kinetic scheme of the first figures in the second row, left – moreover reproduced numerous times by Raphael – can be ascribed to the *effacé* and *croisé* of academic dance in the early 1800s, in the relationship between the arms and legs and the near-frontal orientation of the chest (see p. 142).

Modern Technique and the New Generation

The two images below compare two protagonists of French dance during the late 1700s, at a time when each was at the pinnacle of his repute: Auguste Vestris, son of Gaetano Vestris, in 1781; and Pierre Gardel, younger brother of Maximilien Gardel (who was *maître de ballet* at the Paris Opera from 1781 until his untimely death in 1787), portrayed in the early 1790s.

The younger Vestris is depicted here in a daring thrust: his heel is lifted away from the floor as much as possible, his leg is raised to a right angle, and his torso is precariously off-balance toward the back. Both knees are strongly extended, and his waist – the "center" – is perfectly placed on the supporting base, that is, over the weight-bearing foot. This clearly is a movement demanding great discipline, mastered only after much practice.

Here to the left is Pierre Gardel, eminent representative at the Paris Opera of the *sérieux* genre, in an engraving by Carrée, after a painting by Dutertre (early 1790s). By now, we have travelled far from the high, plumed headdresses of the *Ancien Regime* and the gestural majesty that had been associated with this form of academic tradition and with Noverre's ballets. From the flourish of the cape, the short garment and the flowing hair, one can discern a fresh dynamism in the *noble-héroïque* genre. The loosely-worn hair is new for this genre, as is the extra-canonical positioning, which just in these years would be defined as "*attitude-arabesque*" and later, simply *arabesque* (see p. 137).

The Emancipation of Female Dancing in the Late 1700s

In 1804, in his *Lettres sur la Danse, sur les Ballets et les Arts* (Vol. IV, letter no. XIV, p. 81), Noverre underlines the great changes that had occurred in the area of women's dancing beginning in the late 1700s. After having remained in a subordinate position for more than a century – caused in part by the long, cumbersome dresses, but even more by the norms imposed by decorum – women's dancing now appears to have achieved parity with men's dancing.

> Nevertheless, the dance at that time offered more talents among men than women. The exact opposite is true today. The beautiful sex prevails; triumphant, it struggles with force, vigor and talent against the men; and the women place on the scales of judgment a considerable weight in their favor.

From this poetic image, below, etched in 1799, we can see how the adjustment of women's costumes to the fashions of the revolutionary period favored a broadening of movement and a freer exhibition of the body. Mademoiselle Parisot seems here more like a figure of the imagination than of reality. Her body expresses such lightness as to seem weightless. And this impression is heightened by the garland that so poetically encircles her head.

Between Athleticism and Poetry: Dance in the Napoleonic Era

Positional geometry and broad strokes of movement also characterize this lovely image from 1810 (below, left), property of the Bibliothèque de l'Opéra de Paris, which replicates Armand Vestris and Fortuna Conti Angiolini in the ballet *I Contadini tirolesi* (The Tyrolean Peasants) by G. Rossi. As regards technique, there is little difference between the two dancers; their positions are nearly identical. In both, the toes of the foot raised in the air are lengthened and perfectly aligned with the leg, which is also extended. The linear geometry of the legs is consistent with the perfect shaping of the arms, which are raised well above the head, forming the same oval that Winckelmann theorized to be the ideal (curved) line of beauty. The thrust of the torso and indeed of the entire body is equaled by that of the foot that touches the ground, with its heel detached so far from the floor as to give the impression that the dancers are literally on the tips of their toes.
The need to impress the public with athletic upward thrusts and fresh new feats was among the main objectives of this new generation. And it was precisely at this time that they were experimenting with a rise to the tips of the toes. In 1813, Geneviève Gosselin (who was to die prematurely in 1817) astonished the public by raising herself "sur les orteils" (on the toes), as would later be said. After her, various danseuses would experiment with this practice (Amalia Brugnoli Samengo and Maria Taglioni, et al), until the technique of *relevé sur les orteils* finally acquired its solidity and a rational method of study between the late 1820s and early 1830s.
The image of *The Tyrolean Peasants* also offers confirmation of practices that had already been consolidated inside the Paris Opera relating to the portrayal of characters and the hierarchy of roles.
Despite the fact that the costumes and title recall a specific setting (Tyrol), the protagonists dance in a rigorous technical-academic style. The stroke of modernity bestowed by the particular positioning of the arms in spiral form recalls the most advanced lines of academic dance, as shown here below, right, in an illustration from *The Code of Terpsichore* (London, 1828) by Carlo Blasis.

The New Virtuosity

Heels forcefully detached from the floor; legs raised to right angles and so straight as to appear like a T-square; twisting torsos and arching well above waist level – these are some of the elements conquered by the new "modern" dance.
In this image by Louis Duport, dating back to 1806 and reproduced on the pre-frontispiece of Joseph Berchoux's book *La Danse, ou les Dieux de l'Opéra*, technical challenge is pushed toward the acrobatic, but without sacrificing elegance – that is, the proportional clarity based on the principles of classical art and imposed by the Académie Royale. The legs here are so straight as to resemble a compass needle; the arms frame the head, drawing an elegant oval. This is the aesthetic line that would pry its way through between the late 1700s and early 1800s, for which the emblematic phrase by Pierre Gardel, "Be painters", was considered its aesthetic manifesto.

O Chute épouvantable et digne de mémoire!
Le Parterre aussitôt proclame la victoire.
Chant II.

LA DANSE,
OU
LES DIEUX DE L'OPÉRA,
POËME,
PAR J. BERCHOUX.

A PARIS,
CHEZ GIGUET ET MICHAUD, IMP.-LIBRAIRES,
RUE DES BONS-ENFANS, N°. 34.
M. DCCC. VI.

Turning the Back on the Public: Dance Positions Inspired by Neoclassical Art

These images below summarize the substantial transformations sustained by dance during the first decade of the 19th Century and demonstrate the influence that the official iconographic models exerted on the formulation of new figures that would expand the repertory of poses and positioning in academic dance.
In particular, the images highlight the analogies – in the general arrangement of the body and also its relation to space – between the didactic drawings from Carlo Blasis' manual, *Traité élémentaire, theorique et pratique de l'Art de la danse* (Milan, 1820) and these late 18th Century figures by Canova, which were inspired by the Herculaneum *Dancers*.
A position with the back turned toward the spectator prevails in all the figures, and the self-absorbed attitudes of the Herculaneum *Dancers* are transformed into difficult technical movement, which is masked with elegance and grace. In Canova's paintings (Possagno, Italy, 1798-99), this grace is charming and slightly mischievous; in the figures realized by Blasis, it is a grace understood to be a distinctive mark of academic dance.

Continuity, Development and the Reinterpretation of Tradition during the 19th Century

The First Pointe Shoes

During the 1780s, footwear for female dancers was to undergo a profound modification. On page 144, Marie-Madeleine Guimard was shown in an illustration from 1785 wearing very low footwear, tied at the ankle with laces similar to those on sandals introduced through Greek-style fashion. Not only did this style not change during the decade of the Revolution, but it would in fact be consolidated, the shoe assuming a more tapered shape in keeping with the latest fashion trends.
The images reproduced on this and following page document the manufacture of street shoes between the late 1810s and the mid-century.
The blue slippers worn by Laure Bro in this homonymous painting by Théodore Géricault (below) date back to ca. 1818. The Greek-style shoes are perfectly in keeping with her dress, which is in Imperial style, as we see from the high waist, raised to just below breast-level.

In this fashion sketch published in 1829 in the *Petit Courrier des Dames* (right), we see that shoe styles have not yet changed, in respect to the early years of the century. Greek-style laces and an enclosed, tapered form are still current.
The street shoes below (left) date back to 1820 and 1840, respectively, and they are on display at the Fashion Museum at the Residenzschloss in Ludwigsburg. The laces, although half-hidden inside the shoe, nevertheless still retain echoes of Greek-style fashion.

The three black and white photographs below show Emma Livry's dance shoe (1860), from the collection of the Musée de l'Opéra in Paris. As we see, the shoe reproduces fashion footwear with utmost exactitude, with the exception of the little stitching around the toes, the function of which was to prevent the fabric from being cut by the wooden planks of the stage.
Interior reinforcement is still missing from this shoe and would only be introduced toward the end of the century.

This very interesting image, published in 1810 in the periodical *Le Bon genre*, summarizes all of the elements that characterize theatrical and social dancing of the early 1800s.
The ballet master, following traditional practice, plays the violin. The couple and the two youthful figures practicing their exercises are all executing movements in the latest dance styles. The positioning of the female partner is similar to that of Giambologna's *Mercury* statue, which was quite in vogue at the time and was soon to be immortalized by Blasis in his manual. The youth facing back in *grand plié* and the girl, also with her shoulders turned and with her leg raised to the side at 90°, both demonstrate the highly specialized training that was required for social dancing. And the deep *plié* testifies to the existence of this movement, of which Maria Taglioni writes in her diaries.
Finally, note that, as in the social balls, the slippers for preparatory training were soft and very tight-fitting.

The Latest Echoes of Fashion in Ballets from the First Half of the 19th Century

As we have seen (on pp. 50-59), in the first half of the 18th Century, ballet costumes had gradually become fixed in a conventional style, the basis of which – particularly for the women – was a reworking in theatrical scales of fashionable dress. The process of rendering costumes more in keeping with both the character and the scene was not easy even for the most "modern" costume designers, like Louis-René Boquet for Noverre's ballets. Common practice imposed a representative role on the costume, hence a wealth of fabrics, ornamentation and beautiful headwear, all in keeping with a concept of ballet as being spectacular. The verisimilitude already advocated by Noverre in his 1760 *Lettres sur la Danse et sur les Ballets* would have to wait until the affirmation of neoclassical aesthetics and the diffusion of Greek-style fashion before it could be applied to the exterior image of the dancer.
In the 1820s, changes in fashion – this time resulting from the Restoration (1814-15) – were again to affect the shaping of costumes, which, even if only for a brief time, faithfully followed the patterns created by the new stylists for women of high society. This trend was to progressively decline, however, as the links to the past slowly loosened their grip.
Thus, the case of *Cinderella* (Paris Opera, 1823), costumed as an elegant lady, can be considered a significant descendent of a tradition that had held sway in ballet for over a century. In the new supernatural creatures of a fantastical vein that would be asserted during the Romantic age (*Sylphides, Ondines, Wilis*), priority was given to the harmony between, on the one hand, the character's exterior image and inner nature, and on the other, her sentiments and adventures, rather than attempting to recreate an implausible authenticity. The new *Spirits* of flight, the *Elves* and the supernatural female characters – the conceptual heirs of *Flora* and *Zephyr* – were embodied by graceful danseuses dressed in clothing that was as light and insubstantial as the character's nature was indeterminate and elusive.
The new direction that women's dancing was taking, together with the breadth of conquests in male dance technique and the athletic lifts of the new *pas de deux*, required a costume that was generally freer and lighter, particularly as regards the legs. The tutu created (presumably) by Eugène Lami, compliant to the expressive and technical needs of the new female protagonists, was rapidly standardized into a sort of uniform, the role of which was comparable to that of the *panier* in costumes of the 18th Century.
In this phase of ballet's development, a costume's reference to its own historical and cultural context was more or less evident depending on the historical consistency of the ballet's plot and the interpretive choices made by the choreographer. Yet more authentic were the costumes made for dances of a "national character", even if the presence of characterizing elements depended on the equilibrium between sentiments, a character's adventures and the local "color", as established by the choreographer.

The Influence of Greek-Style Fashion on Ballet Costumes

These two images compare Mademoiselle Clotilde, portrayed in 1797 dressed as Calypso from *Télémaque dans l'île de Calypso* by Pierre Gardel (Paris Opera, 1790), and the Roman copy of the original 4th-Century B.C. bronze *Diana the Huntress*, from the Musée du Louvre in Paris.
Evident in the image of the dancer is the inspiration provided by the statue, whose appearance, according to the chronicles, was carefully reproduced down to the finest detail. The Greek sandals and short, fluttering dress reflect the profound upheaval that was shaking up dance around the beginning of the French Revolution. This trend was to be short-lived, but it would leave a long-lasting mark nonetheless, inasmuch as it was to contribute to the decline of the traditional technical domination of male dancing over that of the female.
Quite interesting here is the way in which the artist has adapted the positioning of the statue to dance movement, but without altering the way in which the legs are set. In the figure at the bottom, *Achille à Scyros* (Paris Opera, 1806), property of the Bibliothèque de l'Opéra de Paris, the costumes, movements and gestures all provide further evidence of French style during the Napoleonic era.

The Imperial Style in Costumes and Technique of the Early 1800s

Returning to the image of Armand Vestris and Fortunata Conti Angiolini in the ballet *I Contadini tirolesi* (The Tyrolean Peasants), which has already been discussed on p. 156, what strikes the eye as regards the attire is the combining of elements derived from traditional Tyrolean costumes (the colors, apron, multicolored suspenders and fluttering ribbons) with a structure that was fashionable during the Napoleonic era: the high waist and low neckline, as seen in the girl's costume, and Vestris' shirt and Titus-style hairdo. This choice is consistent with the movement, in which the performers, set against a rather vaguely accentuated national style, display an academic approach typical of the Opera's new "modern school".
As can be deduced from *The Code of Terpsichore*, published by Carlo Blasis in London in 1828 (see p. 156, right), the arm position of the young Tyrolean man reproduces one of the new *arabesque* figures in style at that time. This abstract concept related only to the main solo roles however, inasmuch as other images from the ballet show dancers busy with movements that are more in tune with the general atmosphere of the dance.

The Latest Echoes of Fashion in Ballet of the 1820s

A clear reference to the latest fashion trends is discernible in the costume worn by the protagonist in *Cendrillon* (Cinderella), a ballet by Albert (François Decombe), which took to the stage of the Paris Opera in 1823.
This reference is easily confirmed by comparing the image of Émilie Bigottini (below, left) in the ballet's title role with the costume illustration published in 1823 in the French fashion review *Costume Parisien* (below, right). The shape of *Cinderella*'s dress reproduces the horizontal cut of the neckline of the French model and, to certain extent, also the styling of the wide hat from the fashion review. In both of these documentations – one relating to ballet and the other to 19th-Century fashion – note that the level of the juncture between the bodice and skirt has not yet reached waist-level, as it will just a few short years later.
Fashion consciousness is also evident in costumes designed for male dancers in this and other ballets staged during those same years and worn either by the same Albert or by that other star of the Paris Opera, Antoine Paul. Moreover, in the costume for the *Prince* in *Cinderella* (below, left), it is hard to ignore the reflections of Gothic and Renaissance revivalism, which, having been introduced by the Directory of 1795, was to have a wide following in all of the arts (consider *The Last Kiss of Romeo and Juliet*, by Francesco Hayez [1823], or yet earlier, Ingres' 1814 painting *Gianciotto Discovers Paolo and Francesca*).

Nudity: a Freedom Gained

As we have seen in the figures on pages 155-164, with the coming of the French Revolution, the female body was to be revealed with its contours in view. This was an adaptation of costumes to the newest fashions, which rejected the corset, the fan and the precious fabrics, in favor of fluttering, transparent fabrics, covered by wide, wrap-around cashmere shawls (see fig. lower left). For the female dancer, lighter materials would allow her to lift her legs to the same level as the men could do and to develop the height and length of her jump – in sum, to bridge the wide gap that separated women's dancing from men's dancing.

Above, left: the *bayadère* Constance Gosselin in 1817, in a reprise of Spontini's opera *Fernand Cortez* (1809). Gosselin's partner at the Paris Opera in 1817 was Carlo Blasis.
Above, right: Émilie Bigottini in the role of *Folly* from *Carnaval de Venise,* by Louis Milon (Paris Opera, 1816).
Left: *Madame Récanier*, portrayed in 1805 by F. P. S. Gérard, wearing a soft cashmere shawl (Musée Carnavalet, Paris).

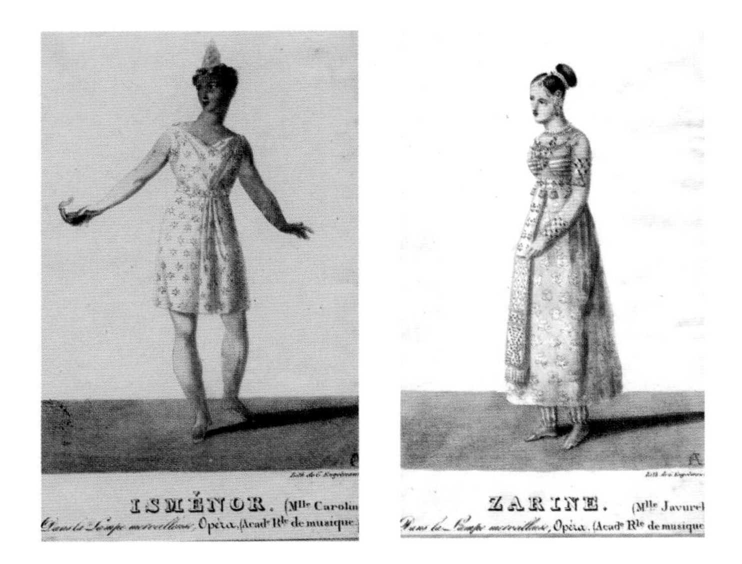

This was a freedom, which, once gained, would not be relinquished. While at the end of the 1820s, popular fashion in women's clothing was to return to wide dresses and hems down to the floor, in dance, neither would skirt hems be lowered again, nor would the costume again be weighted down.

The images on this page display an intriguing transparency, and parts of the body are visibly exposed. During the early 1820s, this applied both to dancers and lyric singers, before later becoming the sole prerogative of dance.

Above are two characters from the opera *La Lampe merveilleuse* (Paris Opera, 1822): the sopranos *Isménor*, Genie of the lamp, and *Zarine*, sister to Aladdin. Below are the well-known dancer Émilie Bigottini in the *pas gracieux* from the same opera and a female *Warrior* from the ballet in the opera *Pharamond* (Paris Opera, 1825).

From *Zephyrs* to the Winged Maidens of Romantic Ballet

Among the elements that characterize Romantic ballet, the winged figure occupies a front row seat. Lithographs, drawings and costume sketches from the first half of the 19th Century show wings of various dimensions, shapes and origins (bird, butterfly, et al), often either connected to demonic aspects (the *Devils* in Blasis' 1835 *Mephistopheles* come to mind) or, more often, evocative of a supernatural poetic condition (*Cupids, Sylphides, Giselle*).
Of all these figures, the one so imprinted upon the collective imagination as to have become *the* primary symbol of Romantic ballet is the ethereal maiden with delicate butterfly wings.
The wings reproduced in historical images do not, however, all take the same form: while *Giselle* is generally represented with classical, fan-shaped wings, a *Sylphide* wing often has such an elongated form that it becomes nearly rectangular, and, like a peacock's wing, it has an eye on it.
While *Giselle*'s wings could be interpreted as a symbol of the soul (in Greek, butterfly and soul are synonymous), those of the *Sylphide* are presumably a result of the transformation and re-contextualization of the iconographic traditions from 18th-Century ballet, comparable to the previously-mentioned conversion in Romantic chords of the *arabesque à deux bras*.
Butterfly wings were already present, as we have seen, in 17th-Century *ballets de cour* – in the iconography of the *Hours* (see p. 42) and in Claude Gillot's costumes for the *opéra-ballet Les Éléments* (see p. 52) – a clear sign of the influence of the iconography codified by Raphael for the *Hours*. With the diffusion of Neoclassicism and the return to Raphael's aesthetic models, the *Hours* represented in the *Banquet of the Gods* at the Villa della Farnesina in Rome became fashionable once again, as did the series of *Hours* originally drawn by Raphael and then reproduced by painters such as Giovanni Sanguinetti in the early 1800s. So it is no coincidence that Louis-René Boquet, in his neoclassical revisit of ballets by Noverre, would have thought to give greater prominence to the winglets inserted into the headdresses and sleeves of the *Zephyrs* from the 1760s, transforming these into symbols that were both conspicuous and consistent with the character's new style of dancing.

A New Prominence for Wings

These images record the transformation of the *Winds* designed by Boquet for Noverre's ballets – from the early 1760s Rococo versions to the neoclassical versions of the 1780s, which are nearer to the iconography from the figurative arts. On the left is *Zephyr*, from the ballet *Psyché* (from the seventh of the eleven volumes given by Noverre to Stanislaw II August of Poland in 1766); on the right, the *Zephyr* from the second of two volumes presented by Noverre to Gustav III of Sweden in 1791.

As can readily be seen in this costume sketch for *Boreas*, the transformation of the costume finds its equivalent in the different poses in which the figures appear; and the increased wingspan corresponds to movement that is both spatially and dynamically expanded. In this neoclassical version, *Boreas* is similar to the Zephyrs that appear in paintings and fountains as followers of Aeolus, and he has large vibrating wings.

From Classical Mythology to the Fantastical World of Romantic Ballet

The iconographic model for *Zephyr* codified in the late 1700s was to converge in the early 1800s with the various versions of the Zephyr and Flora myth choreographed by Charles-Louis Didelot (1812), Jean Coralli (1824) and, in a reprise of Didelot's creation, by Jean Rousset (1828). The exterior aspects of these two divinities from classical mythology were thus established: a small, ultra-light tunic in Greek style for *Zephyr*, leaving his chest half-bare; and for *Flora*, a neoclassical-style dress adorned with simple floral decorations scattered over her short skirt and on her head, in the form of a small crown.

The image here to the left shows Adelaide Mersy and Jean Rousset in *Zefiro e Flora*, performed at the Pergola Theater in Florence in 1828.
In the group of five dancers (below) from E. A. Théleur's *Letters on Dancing* (London, 1831), *Flora* and *Zephyr* are at the extremities (left and right, respectively), recognizable by the above-mentioned conventional attributes of their costumes.
Between *Flora* and *Mercury* is *Psyche*, whose wings are similar to those of *Zephyr*.

The Metamorphosis of the 18th-Century Sylphide

In 19th-Century ballet, the assimilation of the *Sylphide* costume into that of the *Zephyr* can be determined by the analogous aerial nature of the two characters and by the interpretation of the *Sylphide* as being pure *elementary spirit*.
Such an interpretation was, however, already present in 18th-Century lyric theater – as in the epic pastoral *Zaïs* by Jean-Philippe Rameau and Louis de Cahusac (1748), with its *Sylphides* and *Zephyrs* – and in German literature, as well (Christoph Martin Wieland, for example, and Goethe). But in ballet, this was to take on an interesting classical reading: in Noverre's *The Judgment of Paris* (1751), in which, as in classical mythology, *Sylphs* and *Sylphides* appear as followers of Juno (understood to be *Iuno Cœlestis*).
The display of Boquet's costume sketches from the early 1760s in the collection at the University of Warsaw Library grants us the opportunity to analyze Noverre's interpretation of these creatures, as well as the external traits attributed to them by his costume designer. As followers of Juno, the *Sylphs* and *Sylphides* wear conventionally elegant costumes that are appropriate for their roles as royal attendants, while the decorations are inspired by symbols of the goddess herself: the feathers from Juno's sacred animal, the peacock, and clouds, as a reference to the queen's celestial role. On the whole, however, the costumes present strong affinities to that of the *Zephyr* reproduced on page 170, left.

Zb. król. vol. 804 – k. 08

Zb. król. vol. 804 – k. 07

This image of Caroline Brocard as a *Sylphide* in *La Mort du Tasse* by Louis-Jacques Milon (1821) represents a very interesting case, as it documents the free employment of traditional iconographic elements, which is very characteristic of this transitional period. Brocard wears a very light, sheer blue dress with an Empire cut, covered with small stars, and with a small crown of stars instead of a headdress, while elongated wings with a large peacock feather eye in the center issue forth from behind her back. Evident here is the convergence of diverse iconographic elements taken from the *Nymph of the Night* (or *Nymph of the Sky*) and the neoclassical *Zephyr*, which we see documented below in a costume sketch by Louis-René Boquet from 1791 (which is identical to his 1766 design) and in the image of Antoine Paul in a reprise of Didelot's *Zephyr and Flora.*

Vol II, n. 110

The Romantic **Sylphide**

This renowned painting from 1834 by François Gabriel Guillaume Lépaulle portrays Maria Taglioni and her brother Paolo in the opening scene from the ballet *La Sylphide*, created in the same year, to music by Jean Schneitzhöffer, by their father Filippo Taglioni for the Paris Opera.

The painting provides the most evocative testimony as to the transformation of the *Sylphs* and *Sylphides* – air spirits – into the Romantic *Sylphides*. Taking inspiration from the 1822 story by Charles Nodier, *Trilby, ou le lutin d'Argail* (Trilby, the Fay of Argyle), Filippo Taglioni's *Sylphide* has acquired a human connotation, together with a capacity to demonstrate feelings. Her ethereal nature is revealed in the transparency of her wings – similar to those of a dragonfly – and in the symbolic absence of shoes, the levity of her apparently weightless body and, finally, in the impalpability of her dress, which, like Flora's, seems bereft of edges. The penetrating gaze and vigilant attitude, and the slight tension that pervades her body represent love and devotion, but also the temptation of the forbidden dream, creating a strong contrast to "reality", represented here by the interior of a house full of objects that recall the everyday life from which young *James* dreams of escape.

Taglioni's *La Sylphide*, which was to inspire the Danish choreographer August Bournonville in 1836, remains one of the ballets most representative of the Romantic movement in dance. The story of the young Scotsman James, who, on what should be his wedding day, chases a sprite though the forest, leaving all responsibility behind, reflects the interior contrasts and hidden aspirations typical of Romantic literature. While Lépaulle's painting examines the two performers through penetrating eyes – digging into the hidden-most corners of their souls – another iconographic testimony, the nearly coeval book *Les Beautés de l'Opéra, ou Chefs-d'oeuvre lyriques*, published in 1845 by Théophile Gautier, Jules Janin and Philarète Chasles, with drawings by Jules Collignon, presents the ballet under a different light, that of the fable. In the image on this page, Collignon accentuates the story's poetic and fantastical aspects. The refined stylization of the figures, their levity and grace, the sinuosity of their lines and the unrealistic curves of these "little sirens" all recall the style of book illustrations used for imaginary fables. As Gautier writes, "That is the great merit of well-told tales; the more impossible they be, the more tempted are we to believe in them." James is chasing his dream.

This evocative illustration from the same book, *Les Beautés de l'Opéra*, takes us into the sad adventures that signal the end of the *Sylphide*'s existence and the shattering of *James'* dream. At the lower right, among the rocks of a fabled forest, we see the treacherous *Witch* who offers the young man the scarf of magical powers with which *James* would finally be able to catch the elusive spirit. But alas, the poisoned scarf causes the *Sylphide*'s wings to fall off, robbing her of her essence. According to the text, "James remains alone in the world; his beautiful dream has slipped away forever, his sweet vision has vanished, never to return. The Sylphides have carried away their sister, expired like a flower broken off before evening."

The image expresses clearly the four essential elements of the ballet: Evil (the witch), through deformity, old age and a downward bending of the body; the disillusioned dream, through *James'* prostration; reality, expressed by the Scottish clothing; and the unreality and evanescence of the dream, through the ethereal flying figures.

Between Imagination and Reality: Tradition and New Aesthetic Lines in *Giselle*

Giselle

The images presented on the following pages offer a reflection on several aspects of the ballet *Giselle*, which was first staged at the Paris Opera on June 28, 1841. The story was written by Théophile Gautier, and the libretto by Jules-Henri Vernoy de Saint-Georges; the choreography was by Jean Coralli and Jules Perrot; the music by Adolphe Adam; the stage designs by Pierre-Luc-Charles Ciceri; and the costumes were designed by Paul Lormier.
The story of the peasant girl named Giselle is as well-known as the ballet itself, so it will suffice here to summarize it quite briefly: Giselle, just fifteen years old, falls in requited love with a young nobleman, Albrecht, who, in order to be close to her, stays in a cabin across from her house, disguising himself as a peasant named Loys. But the local Gamekeeper Hilarion, now a rejected lover, exposes the deceit, as well as the nobleman's impending marriage to a noblewoman, after which, the maiden dies of a broken heart. The arrival of death before matrimony transforms Giselle into a Wili, one of the ghost-spirits that roam the woods, attracting wayfarers into a diabolical dance to the death. But her passionate love for Loys (Albrecht) succeeds in prolonging his dance until dawn, and the youth is saved, and returned to his "true" love.
Despite having intrinsic picturesque and fantastical elements typical of Romantic aesthetics – the medieval castle on a cliff, the supernatural creatures, the mysterious, nocturnal atmosphere and the absence of boundaries between reality and dream – the ballet presents certain ties to 18th-Century tradition that bear witness both to a continuity with the past and to an updating of concepts and practices used during the century before. The aesthetic changes and new expressive horizons that had characterized ballet from the 1780s until the Restoration did not expel those fantastical elements of mythological origins, but instead, as Charles Nodier also writes, redirected these toward new sources and themes. For this reason, various traditional elements survived, recoated with a Romantic patina or converted into more "modern" equivalents. The transformation of the *arabesque à deux bras* has already been noted, as has the assimilation of *Zephyr* wings by the new *Sylphides*. At this point, our attention is drawn to some symbolic elements contained in the portrait of *Giselle* on page 181, which induces reflection on both the grape harvest theme and the dance with a tambourine from the first act. Another element still to be addressed is the Bacchanal from the tenth scene of Act II of the same ballet.

Between Verisimilitude and Imagination in Giselle

In Act I of *Giselle*, the vagueness of the setting – which is imagined to be some undefined place (perhaps Thüringen or Silesia, but at the same time, in the hills along the Rhine) and is generically ascribable to an indeterminate period centuries ago – offers the stage designer an opportunity to conceive an extraordinarily evocative scenario; the peasant world and its customs are not represented literally, but are instead replaced by the outline of a "reality" that is functional to both the adventure and the characters, and is also in keeping with the tastes of the period.
The following illustrations by Jules Collignon are from the previously-mentioned book published in 1845 by Théophile Gautier, *Les Beautés de l'Opéra*. Observing this image from the first act (below), we can see the determination of stage designer Pierre-Luc-Charles Ciceri to confer credibility onto the setting; but even more, it informs us as to how much the imaginary, fantastical aspect of the second act would reverberate back into the first part of the story, bestowing a certain poetry upon a common adventure of love and deceit, and transporting the spectator into a timeless dimension.
The architecture here is that traditionally used: a trellised house on the left and, across from it, the straw-roofed cabin where the duke Albrecht, in the guise of a farmer named Loys, takes lodging. In the background, a feudal residence sits atop an impervious rise, evoking a world as distant from the circumstances of the humble Giselle as are those of the real Albrecht. The proscenium is framed by a natural arc of trees that delineates the space of the action and contributes to the enchanted tone to the scene.

GISELLE

Giselle est le premier ballet que Carlotta Grisi ait dansé à l'Opéra, où elle avait débuté par ce pas si brillant de *la Favorite*, qui est encore un des plus beaux fleurons de sa couronne chorégraphique. On se souvenait bien d'avoir vu, il y a quelques années, à la Renaissance, une charmante enfant qui jouait un rôle dans une pièce intitulée *Zingaro;* mais l'on ne savait pas si c'était une danseuse ou une chanteuse, car elle était l'une et l'autre. Une voix fraîche, pure et juste, une danse légère et correcte, de beaux yeux bleus d'une douce naïveté, voilà ce que Carlotta Grisi avait laissé dans la mémoire des gens du monde et des feuilletonistes. *Giselle* la plaça tout d'un coup au premier rang. Un poëte de nos amis trouva dans une légende allemande, pour cette blonde

1.

As the sketches for the original stage design have been lost, it is impossible to determine the depth of Collignon's fidelity to it. But this leaf from *Les Beautés de l'Opéra* is still extremely useful in understanding Ciceri's innovations and grasping the suggestive effect that was used so successfully by the artist in exalting the story's picturesque and fairy-tale aspects. These are the years when architecture was to definitively displace painting; stage sets, which previously had consisted of painted backdrops and wings (see p. 37), were now being constructed using architectural elements and furnishings that articulated the space, rendering the setting more realistic.

Between Verisimilitude and Fashion in Giselle

These two images from *Les Beautés de l'Opéra* illustrate two moments from Act I of *Giselle*: the arrival of Albrecht's fiancée, the princess *Bathilde* (top), and the stirring scene of *Giselle*'s death (bottom).
Observing the figures, we can recognize a fashion trend particular to those years: an interest in costumes made in the mid-to late 16th-Century style of Charles IX-Henry IV. Also apparent, however, is the wide caesura between the characters of the "story" (mimes and extras) and the dancing characters. Giselle's *Friends* (and *Giselle* herself) wear the "modern" costumes of "dancers", an apparent last-minute modification to the project.

The portrait of Carlotta Grisi on the next page (from *Les Beautés de l'Opéra*) shows how the simple, humble costume of the original had become a vaporous tutu, further refined by the small apron and crowned by a dark, low-necked bodice. If, at first glance, the costume in its entirety might recall those of 19th-Century German innkeepers, as portrayed in the previously-cited publication by Braun & Schneider, other elements diverge decisively. The costume is extraordinarily similar to those of other protagonists of the era in operas and ballets staged at the Paris Opera (such as Zerlina in *Don Giovanni* or Rosina [below, left], from *The Barber of Seville*, both reproduced in *Les Beautés de l'Opéra*). Other elements however merit further reflection. The small apron is a clear reference to the traditional-national costume (see pp. 124 and 218-219), which serves to place *Giselle* in a peasant context. The shape of the bodice, on the other hand, with its very deeply-cut horizontal neckline, is borrowed from the evening dresses that had been in vogue for over a decade and had already been used in previous ballets. The final result is a free aggregation of diverse elements that contribute to form a very graceful entirety of fantasy that is perfectly concordant with the ballet's poetic and fantastical dimensions, but at the same time, also sensitive to the qualities of femininity and grace possessed by Carlotta Grisi, the Italian ballerina with the romantic blue eyes. The costume sketch below, right, taken from an 1829 edition of *Petit Courrier des Dames*, shows how the peasant girl costume that Giselle wears in the first act is in keeping with current fashion: the neckline is cut horizontally and low enough to leave the shoulders completely exposed, just as in the costume here for the lyrical singer *Rosina* in Rossini's *The Barber of Seville*.

CARLOTTA GRISI.

Classical Recollections in Giselle

The first act of *Giselle* takes place during the autumn festival that directly follows the vintage. The objective of Vernoy de Saint-Georges is clearly to create a sort of container for the adventures and provide a pretext for joyous and charming dances. Although the choreography was conceived on modern schemes, it is no coincidence that, in the vintage from the ballet *Giselle*, a connection is recognizable, not only to the settings of coeval *opéras-comiques*, but indeed to the *Autumn* of many 18th-Century *opéras-ballets*. In the portrait of Grisi, even the presence of the stick with a sort of pine cone tip, like a Dionysian thyrsus, while aimed at giving color and realism to the scene, further betrays the memory of a tradition that had been maintained in the applied arts and diffused on a wide scale through handicraft, some of it quite valuable.

As regards the tambourine, which we see here in a print from *Les Beautés de l'Opéra*, the following points merit consideration. Having ascertained that this is neither the *tambour de basque* (Basque tambourine) from *Le Diable boiteux* (Paris Opera, 1836), nor that from *La Gypsy* (Paris Opera, 1839), it can be added that, during the first half of the 19th Century, paintings by artists like Antoine Thomas and Louis Léopold Robert (see p. 197) and the association of the grape harvest to Bacchus, the Bacchanal, the Bacchantes and the dancing Dryads with tambourines of 18th-Century ballet (see pp. 103, right, and 150) had combined to create the stereotyped image of the young girl who dances with tambourine in hand and a vine branch adorning her hair. This model may also have held sway in ballet. In *Giselle*, and also in the later *L'Étoile de Messine* by Pasquale Borri (1861), the tambourines are played by the (female) dancers themselves, not by the musicians, as had been customary. In this regard, note the resemblance of the girl at the right of the print to the French bronze statuette from the same period, reproduced on page 197.

The Bacchanal from "Giselle"

In the second act, a scene occurs that constitutes one of the dramatic pillars of the ballet: the ritual dance of the *Wilis* that brings about the death of *Hilarion*, Giselle's unrequited lover, who has ventured into the forest to mourn at the tomb of his beloved.

In this figure from *Les Beautés de l'Opéra*, the *Wilis* are chasing the unfortunate Gamekeeper, urged onward by their homicidal fervor. In the libretto for *Giselle*, however, the *Wilis* are presented as bacchantes. This is suggested in the quotation from *De l'Allemagne* by Heinrich Heine, reprinted at the beginning of the libretto:

> "... adorned in their wedding gowns, with floral crowns on their heads, brilliant rings on their fingers, the *Wilis* dance in the bright moonlight, like *Elves*; their figures, white as snow, are filled with youthful beauty. They laugh with perfidious joy, they call to you with such seduction and an air scented with sweet promise; how irresistible are these lifeless Bacchantes."

However, while the violence of the Wilis is apparent in the libretto and also in the illustration from *Les Beautés de l'Opéra*, in the annotations of the stage action made by Marius Petipa while observing the ballet and written down in a *répétiteur* (a text arranged for rehearsals and given to the second violinist), the nature and role of these Wili-Bacchantes appear more easily comprehensible.

> Enter Hilarion. Filled with terror, he tries to save himself, chased by the Wilis. They disappear. Myrtha leads them. They force Hilarion to dance. The Bacchanal of the Wilis. Hilarion begins to dance. The Wilis drag him to the back under a tree. Another group. Myrtha orders the Wilis to take Hilarion. He falls to his knees. Myrtha touches him lightly with a branch, he pleads with her, but she refuses. He pleads with her again. She says, "No! No! You must dance, here." Hilarion dances. Myrtha takes him and pushes him toward the Wilis. The dance is feverish. Hilarion begs the sovereign. She again tells him, "No! No!" The Wilis form a circle around Hilarion for a carousel. He goes round together with the Wilis. A satanic smile. He exits turning, upstage toward the peak of the hill. The Wilis push him into the lake, he falls.

Also in the dance of the Wilis from the second act Bacchanal, it is possible to trace a distant echo of classical tradition, with various elements leading back to Greek mythology (the name of the Queen of the Wilis, for example, which is derived from the myrtle, symbol of love) and in particular, to the myth of Orpheus.
In the 18th Century, the myth of Orpheus and Eurydice was used frequently in ballet and lyric opera – from John Weaver's *The Fable of Orpheus and Eurydice* (London, 1718) to *La Descente d'Orphée aux Enfers*, composed by Jean-Georges Noverre during the first phase of his career (1750s), and Christoph Willibald Gluck's *Orfeo ed Euridice* (Vienna, 1762). And it fascinated the public through its poetic balance between fantastical, sentimental and moral elements, and that stirring counter-positioning of life and death which underpins so much of literature and also so many popular tales. As in the Orpheus myth, the Bacchanal from Act II of *Giselle* is a cruel dance of death, in which the deceased maidens transform into executioners, pouring their resentment at having been denied love over men. This concept is clearly gathered from the transcription by Henri Justamant, *maître de ballet* at the Paris Opera in 1868-69. This transcript, property of the Deutsches Tanzarchiv in Cologne, was issued in facsimile in 2008 by publishing house OLMS, edited by Frank-Manuel Peter. Reproduced on the following pages are four of the most important pages describing the Bacchanal, which, beginning with the capture of the unfortunate Gamekeeper, will eventually lead to his death.

In contrast to the music, in which accents are used to highlight the lugubrious atmosphere, in the choreography, the tale's violence is represented not mimically, but symbolically, using vehicles typical of 18th-Century tradition. This is the first figure of the Bacchanal, and the dominant choreographic element is running. The *Wilis* enter running, and *Hilarion* does so too, but he is blocked by several *Wilis* who barricade his path.

179

Bacchanale

quatres willis entre en courant, la moitiée droit devant, et les autres détourne vers leur droite et appelle leurs compagnes

hilarion effaré, pale de frayeur entre en courant il tourne la tête derriere lui et apperçoit des wilis qui le poursuive

des wilis sortant de la coulisse lui barre le chemin il se sauve de l'autre coté, sans faire attention ou il va.

Small circles recur repeatedly in the pages from the manuscript reproduced here, symbolizing the grip of pain and death with which the *Wilis* seize *Hilarion* and force him to dance, until they finally finish him off in the final central circle (see next page), which appears to be some sort of death ritual.
Tossed about from one circle to the next, the misfortunate youth is pushed around cruelly and seized violently time and again, until, in similarity to the myth of Orpheus, he is thrown from the heights of a hill into a lake (see p. 188).

185

La reine fait un signe
les deux wilis pousse hilarion vers les autres qui aussitot forment un rond.

les wilis qui entouren hilarion se donnent les mains et tournent en sautant.
les autres placée en rond font continuellement le même pas que la figure n° 2.

la reine au milieu fait un signe
les deux wilis prenne hilarion et l'entraine dans le rond du coté oposé
il ne sait plus ou il en est

The reader will notice that, in the original transcript, the outline of the skirted characters is standardized, and this applies for both female and male characters, which are distinguishable from each other through the colors used, red and black, respectively. In the figure below, *Hilarion* (at the center of the circle) is represented in black, while the *Wilis* are marked in red.

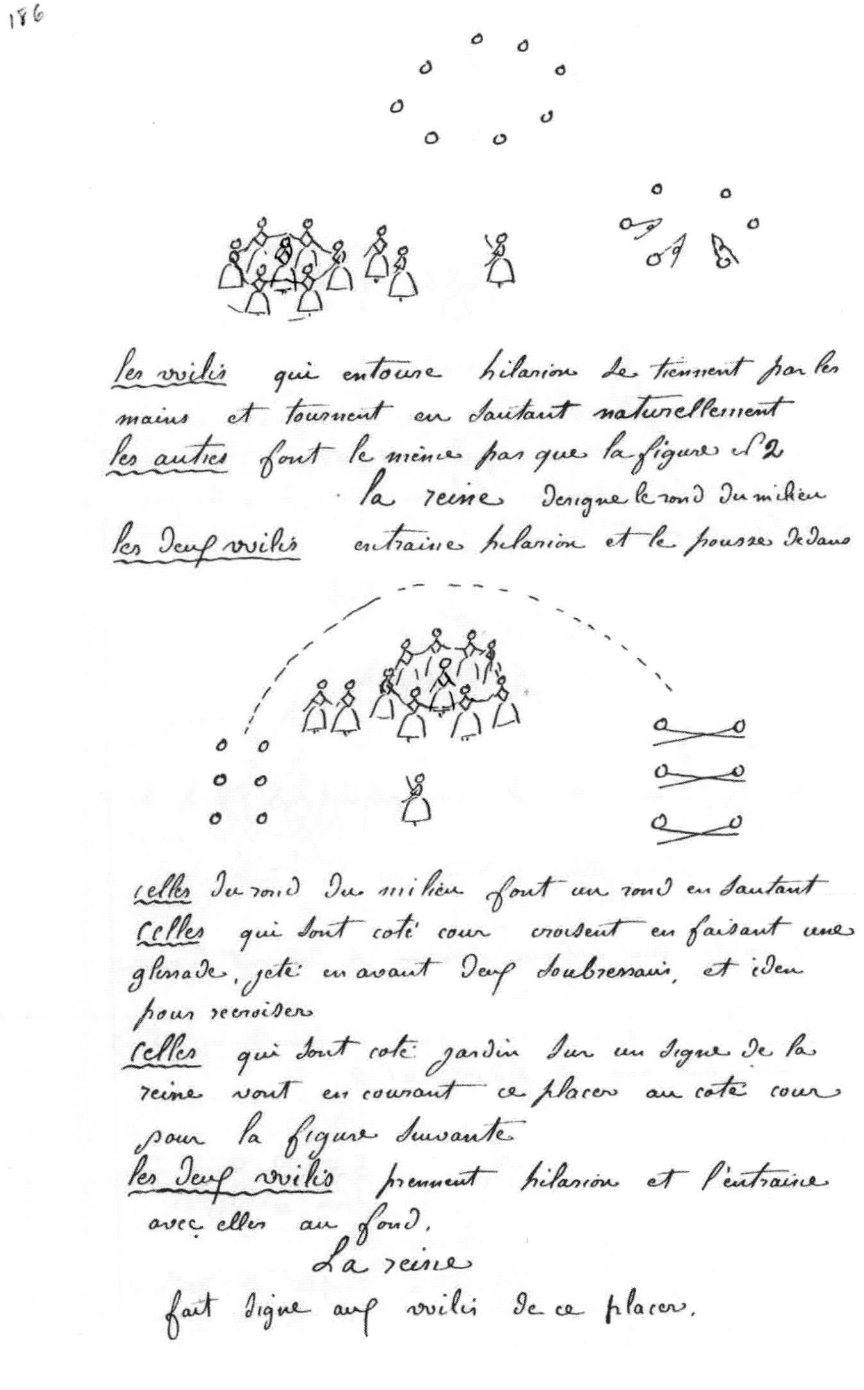

186

les wilis qui entoure hilarion se tiennent par les mains et tournent en sautant naturellement
les autres font le même pas que la figure n° 2
la reine designe le rond du milieu
les deux wilis entraine hilarion et le pousse dedans

celles du rond du milieu font un rond en sautant
Celles qui sont coté cour croisent en faisant une glissade, jeté en avant deux soubresauts, et idem pour recroiser
Celles qui sont coté jardin sur un signe de la reine vont en courant se placer au coté cour pour la figure suivante
les deux wilis prennent hilarion et l'entraine avec elles au fond.
La reine
fait signe aux wilis de se placer.

Visible at the top of this page is the lake into which *Hilarion* will be hurled to his death. The two rising diagonals (downstage to upstage) are very strong semantic signals of drama and, as such, have a value comparable to the diagonal placement of the *Wilis'* at the moment when *Giselle,* deceased but not yet a ghost, leaves her tomb.

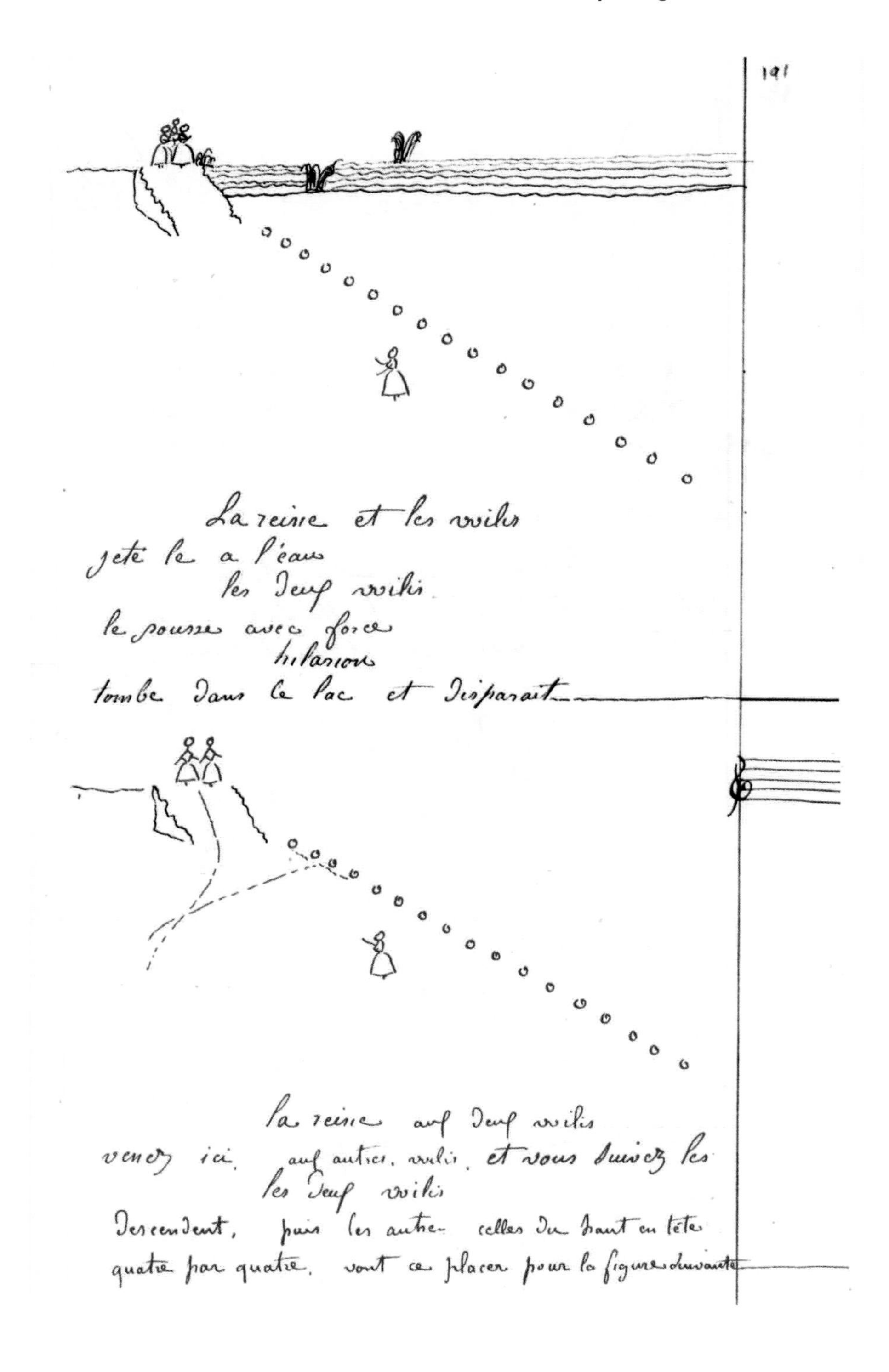

Also this beautiful portrait of Adèle Dumilâtre in the role of *Myrtha, Queen of the Wilis* is filled with symbolism. The *baguette magique* is a branch of rosemary, instead of the verbena prescribed by Gautier in *Les Beautés de l'Opéra*. Rosemary was linked to marriage in some traditions, whereas in 18th-Century ballet, the rose, jasmine and myrtle were all codified as representing love. The young woman is presented not as a cruel queen who sends wayfarers to their deaths, but rather, as *Myrtha the Wili*, or dancing spirit, and a reincarnation of love (even if this love remains unrealized). Her movement is graceful, and her body, nearly entirely visible, is shaped with a rounded grace. Her dress and head are both decorated with delicate roses, like other Romance-era heroines. A wide butterfly wing, symbol of the soul and a distinct trait of the Wilis, peeks out from behind her arm. The visual prominence and perfectly-drawn positioning appear to indicate that the character is not subject to the laws of gravity.
Behind her, a glimpse can be caught of *Giselle*, just leaving her tomb, covered with a veil.

Flying Figures Suspended between Dream and Reality

La Péri

Théophile Gautier is remembered above all for the ballet *Giselle*. But his other creation, *La Péri*, is no less interesting and indicative of the aesthetic orientation of French Romanticism in dance. Gautier wrote the libretto in collaboration with Jean Coralli, who was also the choreographer. The ballet, with music by Friedrich Burgmüller, was premiered at the Paris Opera on July 17, 1843.
This ballet also has a fantastical plot, which, inspired by mythology (Persian this time), develops into an adventure suspended in the spaces between imagination and reality, between aspirations and everyday life, and between love and death – all in the fabled setting of the pasha's palace in Cairo.
Prince Achmet, dissatisfied with the pleasures of the harem, seeks refuge in opium. In his imagination, he is taken to the garden of the Péri (fairies from Persian mythology), where the queen offers him a bouquet of flowers with a star from her diadem in the center; if he kisses this, she will appear. But Achmet's uncertainty makes the queen jealous, and to assure herself of Achmet's love, she turns into reality the mad idea of entering the world of mortals, assuming the form of a slave named Leila, just at the moment, however, when Leila is killed by palace guards.

From here, a series of yet more complicated adventures and ambiguous situations begins, which concludes with Achmet's refusal to return Leila to the pasha. His disobedience lands him in prison, condemned to death. But at the moment of his execution, the prison walls magically vanish, allowing the apparition of splendid clouds, which carry Achmet, inextricably linked to the Péri, into Muslim paradise. The ballet was indeed nearly as successful as *Giselle* – for its lights and colors, its sensuous atmosphere and mysterious vibrations, and for its dimension of fantasy, which placed no borders between dream and reality. The plot, more intricate and contrast-rich than in *Giselle*, called for plenty of mime, but also plenty of dancing; and it had one daring scene that, as Gautier himself relates, had become "as famous as Niagara Falls". The scene is portrayed in a renowned etching, reproduced on the previous page from a German newspaper (1844): it occurs at the end of the *Pas de songe* in Act I, when the *Péri*, as light as a dove's feather, throws herself from the clouds and flies (for a full two meters, apparently) into the arms of her beloved.

In this color image, the *Péri*, embodied as the slave *Leila*, is immortalized in the final moment of the *Pas de l'abeille* (Act II), in which she falls at *Achmet*'s feet, "gasping, exhausted, and smiling within her own fear". The unusual profile position shows how the painter would have understood the comparison with the *Venus* of antiquity proposed by Gautier in *La Presse* (a similarity is also noted to the Aphrodite from the Ludovisi Throne at the Palazzo Altemps in Rome). But above all, it reveals an intention to praise the sensuality of the danseuse, showing her splendid, nearly half-exposed body (shoulders bared, as is the beautiful leg placed in the foreground), and also to play with the double-identity of the protagonist (the slave *Leila* wears the same costume as the fairy *Péri*). As Gautier writes, the *Pas de l'abeille* was inspired by a traditional Egyptian dance of seduction; the dancer, pretending to want to escape from a bee, dispenses with parts of her costume and stays "with a simple voile skirt." With the stars that crown her head, the scanty costume and pink fabric on her abdomen, simulating bare skin, and the chromatic contrast between the semi-transparent muslin skirt and the sky-blue bodice, she certainly bewitched the story-prince *Achmet*; but in real life too, she had all the male heads spinning.

Dance in Italy and the Tradition of the Choreographer-Director

In the first half of the 19th Century, the production of ballets in Italy was quite vast and variegated, and it was characterized by an aesthetic line very different from that of the French. Not much inclined toward fantastical plots, the Italian public followed with great attention the adoption in ballet of historically-based adventures and those of political and/or moral value, which were firmly coupled to a reality that was concrete, recognizable and could be shared.
However, while during the first half of the century, native Italian culture made a mark on ballet that was specific and well-distinguished from that of ballet in France, from the mid-century onward – and particularly after the unification of the nation in 1861 – Italian dance did react to the novelties coming from abroad, incorporating certain structural aspects. *Excelsior*, which will be discussed further on, was the most significant example of the decline of traditional pantomime in favor of pure dance, and of the contamination of the Italian School by an international language. This was a radical change, as, during the first half of the century, mimic gesture and action had covered central roles in the conception and structure of ballets. Nevertheless, as in the political sphere, unity was not to be found in dance. This can be attributed to changes in the public and to the cultural currents that cast precise conditions on artistic production; on top of this, one must add education, which implied a different professional competence for each choreographer (depending on whether a dancer or a mime). In Italy, also the tradition of the choreographer-director in the mold of Noverre was to persist. Luigi Manzotti was to become the most illustrious case in point; but Carlo Blasis remains the most interesting one, for the evidence he provides regarding that concept of ballet as total performance that had initially been experimented with by Noverre.

This drawing by Blasis for *Doctor Faust*'s study (left), from the ballet *Mephistopheles, or the Genius of Evil*, is testimony of the magniloquence of stage structures and the profundity and complexity as regards the use of space, which will be discussed on the following page.

Carlo Blasis, Choreographer-Director

Of great interest in the panorama of Italian ballet in the first half of the 19th Century is *Mephistopheles, or the Genius of Evil*, a "poetic-philosophical *ballo*" in nine scenes, conceived and proposed to the La Scala Theater by Carlo Blasis in 1835, but which only reached the stage three decades later, in Warsaw (1867). What remains from the first version of the ballet are its designs, signed by Blasis and preserved at the Biblioteca del Teatro alla Scala, some examples of which are reproduced here.
The libretto, written by Blasis himself and then published in 1843 in the periodical *La Fama*, was extracted from Goethe's *Faust*, which, after its issue in 1823, had been through several adaptations for ballets and was still to earn yet more interest from choreographers all across Europe.
Blasis' ballet was characterized by a notable complexity as regards the action and the use of scenery, which in a number of scenes, almost turned itself into the main protagonist. Blasis' evident intention was to place himself directly on that long choreographic line which, starting with the *ballet d'action* at La Scala of the early 18th Century, was to remain vibrant for quite some time (as apparent in the *gran ballo Excelsior* and in *Amor*).
Here below, we have the stage design sketch for the second scene (*The Heights of the Haritz Mountains – Sinister Night*), as drawn by Blasis, who was inspired by the fourth *canto* of *Jerusalem Delivered*. The subject is the moment when Doctor Faust descends from the mountain with Mephistopheles and the Witch to accomplish the miracle of his rejuvenation. Warlocks, sorcerers, gypsies and all sorts of horrible monster clamor about the infernal scenario, between the cries of ferocious animals and the sinister whistling of wind, and stupefying bursts of lightning. The gloomy atmosphere is conveyed through a monstrous anthropomorphic representation of nature.

From the figure below, one can see the great lengths to which Blasis went in order to give his creation a coherence as regards the rapport between content and how this was rendered visible. Also evident is the care taken with the smallest details of costumes, which were intended as integral parts of one harmonious entirety. In the figure on the left, *Mephistopheles* is represented wearing a lavish 15th-Century outfit, with a sword at his side and a hat with "cock feathers". On the right, *Doctor Faust* is presented as an old scientist.

On the page below, note how Blasis would make reference to the Italian *grotesque* genre to realize the acrobatic movements of the demons, the damned and the figures rising toward the sky in the final Apotheosis. In the group at the upper right, observe the *grotesque* interpretation of the "pursuit and flight" scheme, which has been discussed on pages 145-148.

Although more recent by half a century, this image below, from the ballet *Amor* by Luigi Manzotti (La Scala, 1886) provides evidence of the persistence in late 19th-Century Italy of the tradition of ballet being seen as "total performance". Evident here is the fundamental role of the scenery and also the lucid manner in which a diversity of dancing styles is presented – both aspects that recall the birth of the *ballet d'action* in the 1700s.
Likewise in this image, taken from the journal *Il Teatro Illustrato* (Special Supplement to issue no. 62, February, 1886), we see a mass of characters onstage in various roles and capacities. Here, we can also recognize the function of using animals, which adds realism and dramatic weight to the *tableau*.

The Stylization of Popular Themes in French Art

In 18th-Century ballet, the process of reproducing themes extracted from the popular world had been subjected to a procedure of purification that, as with the manufacture of porcelain, stripped away the more realistic characteristics in order to offer the public a refined product that was in accord with the tastes of a cultivated and informed spectator.
Even in the 19th Century, although the public had changed (and was often distinctly less refined), ballet attempted neither to portray reality in a faithful manner, nor to describe the characteristics and gestures of its characters in their naturally spontaneous and prosaic aspects. Ballet no longer had much to do with the idealized imitation of nature as proposed in the classical arts, as had been the case in the 18th Century, but rather with needs specific to both theater and ballet itself, as well as the perpetuation of a tradition that had already been consolidated.
This can be gathered from the all-French sampling on the opposite page, selected from the iconographic repertories of the applied arts and ballet.
To begin with the statuettes that reproduce the *Tarantella* (next page, upper and lower left), the terracotta figure, although undated, is attributable to the 1830s or -40s; the female bronze figure is slightly more recent. In the terracotta, together with a series of specific details that were inserted to facilitate the identification of the dance (the dress, gestures, shoes, etc.), note the grand elegance of the features and movements, which certainly do not refer to the popular world. The female bronze figure, on other hand, is part of a couple, her male companion being a precise reproduction of the youthful dancing peasant in Louis Léopold Robert's painting *The Arrival of the Reapers in the Pontine Marshes* (1830), which is displayed at the Musée du Louvre. Unlike her partner, whose gesture and clothes appear to depict rather faithfully those customary in the lower Lazio region of Italy, the stylization in the dancing girl is so accentuated that, not only are the dress and decorations twisted, but also the movement, accompanied unrealistically by the tambourine. The movements have an almost academic grace, and the dress, quite far removed from traditional costumes, seems instead to evoke the Maenads and Pompeian *Dancers*. In both cases (the terracotta and the bronze), we see a certain stylization comparable to that in this painting by Léopold Robert (*Two Girls near Naples*, 1821), reproduced at the lower right.
Comparison between these statuettes and the coeval pair in painted ceramic, manufactured in Naples (upper right), confirms the profound gap between folklore and the cultivated interpretation of popular themes. The gestures in the Neapolitan ceramic have a spontaneity and an emphasis typical of *ballo popolare, or* popular dancing, and the costumes faithfully replicate the styling and colors of traditional costumes.

Stylization in French Ballet

Poetic license and a stylization of gestures and décor are all evident in the protagonist dancers from Jules Perrot's successful ballet, *Catarina ou la Fille du bandit* (London, 1846; Milan, 1847), which is compared here to an image from a mid-19th-Century album of costumes from the Abruzzo region of Italy.
In the image at the lower left, Lucile Grahn, as the ballet's protagonist, is presented as the leader of a group of bandits from the land of Abruzzo, who kidnap the painter Salvator Rosa. In the image at the lower right, *Catarina* dances with her lieutenant, *Diavolino* (Jules Perrot). Comparing the costumes of the two dancers with traditional costumes (here to the left), we see that the differences are substantial. The gestures by Grahn and Perrot, and also their clothing, are the results of traditional characteristics being stylized in a theatrical language. The girl's musket and Abruzzo-style men's hat (below, left), recall her role as the head of group of seasoned bandits; but her attitude – proud and resolute as it is (note the steady gaze and strongly angled position of the body, with her hand on her hip) – has a grace that reveals the nobility of her sentiments and generosity of her gestures, while at the same time, exalting the femininity of the danseuse. Much the same can be said of her partner Jules Perrot, whose costume invokes the setting (note the elegantly-modeled hat and the fashioning of the *ciocia*, traditional shoes from the Ciociaria region in Italy); these references present, more than anything else, picturesque touches of color, just like Grahn's precious, close-fitting jacket, the hat placed at a gracious angle and the elegant shawl on her tutu. In the panorama of 19th-Century ballet, this production was one of many cases of adventures given a "national" setting. The numerous images made available through prints from the era testify as to how the desire to grant authenticity would sometimes be the prevailing interest for the choreographer and costume designer, and how, at other times, the reverse was true, the subject matter acting rather as a pretext. In either case, they all display a pronounced attention to color, which in some cases, even seems to be the main protagonist of the costume.

The Use of Space in 19th-Century Ballet

On this page and the next are two sheets from the transcriptions for the *gran ballo Excelsior*, preserved at the Theater Museum at La Scala. The transcription is by Giovanni Cammarano, principal dancer in the 1883 Parisian version.
The first image, below, relates to the second scene, entitled *Light*, which praises the victory of *Light* over *Obscurantism*, that is, of Knowledge over Ignorance.
While the ballet itself will be discussed further on, our task here is to draw attention to the conception of space and the arrangement of the scenery in ballet between the mid- and late 19th Century.
The drawing is composed of two parts. The front section, representing stage level, shows four transversal lines indicating the placement of the wings. In the back section, note the staircases and practicables that accommodate dancers up to levels that increase in height. As we can also see on pages 223 and 224, the choreography filled the entire space, and it was played out on various levels (naturally, in various ways, as well), from the forestage to the areas far upstage.

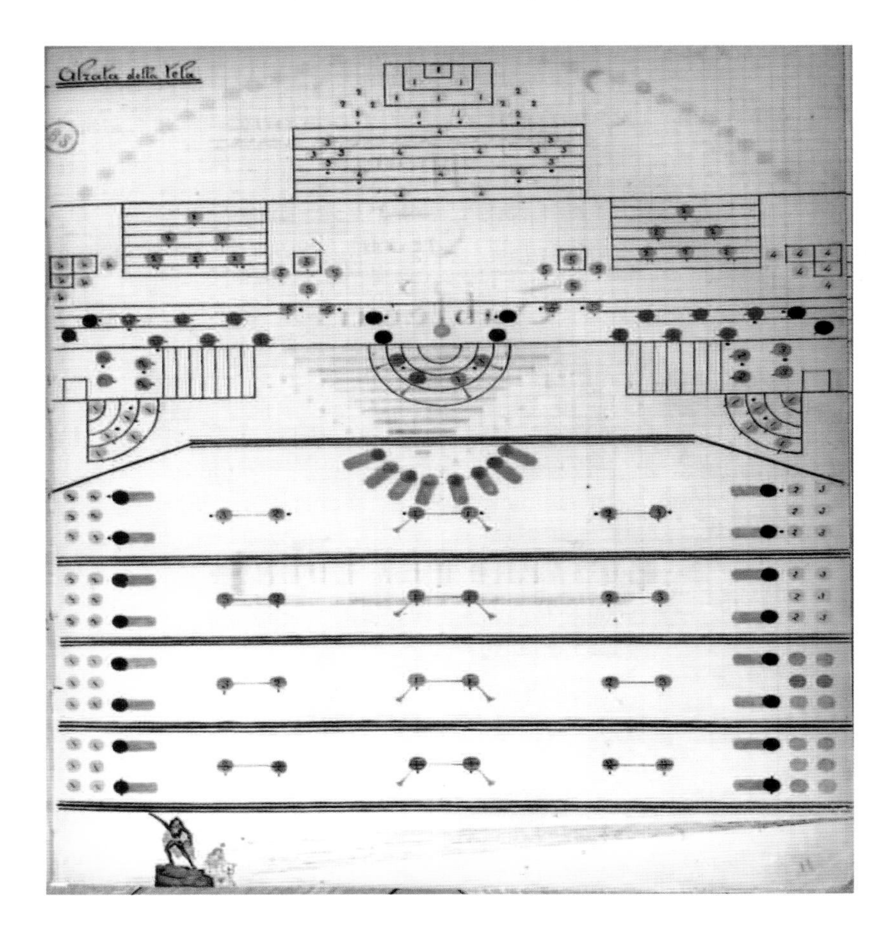

The image below is a page from Giovanni Cammarano's 1883 transcription of the third scene, entitled *The First Steamship*, from the *gran ballo Excelsior*, which was premiered at La Scala on January 11, 1881. The action is set in Germany, on the banks of the Weser River in the early 1700s. Recognizable on the right is the Postilions' Inn; on the left is a tavern. In the Weser (which flows across the center of the page), we see what is left of the unfortunate Denis Papin's invention – the first steamship – which was destroyed by German boatmen in 1707. In the background (at the top), we see the marvelous apparition of New York Harbor, with its ferries and big ships, and a train that streaks across the Brooklyn Bridge, evidence of the importance given in Italian dance to stage technique (*scenotecnica*).

The Union of Body, Mind and Soul: Theory and Practice in the Treatise by Carlo Blasis

Allegory and Graphic Representation as Educational Tools

Carlo Blasis remains one the most prominent figures of 19th-Century dance. His fame is linked not only to his having directed the Imperial Regia Accademia di Ballo (Imperial Royal Academy of Dance) at La Scala (from 1837 to 1850) – which projected a large number of excellent ballerinas onto the international scene – but also to his editorial output. While his *Traité élémentaire théorique et pratique de l'Art de la danse*, published in Milan in 1820, has already been cited, here we would like to highlight his more strictly theoretical publications – in particular, the text *L'uomo fisico, intellettuale e morale* (Physical, Intellectual and Morale Man).
This text, issued in its definitive form in 1857, represents the culminating moment of Blasis' intellectual activity, in which the *Maestro* offers an overall view of his aesthetic vision for dance. Of particular interest for present-day readers are the illustrated tables, a selection from which is reprinted here. Two central aspects of his aesthetic and didactic viewpoint are to be extracted from these: first, the importance of graphic representation, understood as a vehicle for the immediate communication of concepts, and second, his efforts to create a classification of mimic gestures expressing the various passions.
In the allegoric table on the following page – the first of the book – the author illustrates, by way of images, the equilibrium in man between his material aspect (the five senses that form the upper frame), his moral aspect (central group) and his intellectual aspect (figure at the bottom).
In the upper crown (from left to right) are: taste, smell, vision, hearing and touch (depicted as union-love).
At the center, with a club (symbol of physical strength), is Man, with his hand on his heart (symbolizing moral strength); he is surrounded by the passions: *violent passions* (the Fury, kneeling in front, with serpents and a dagger), *calm passions* (center, standing), *painful passions* (to the right of Man), and *pleasurable passions* (in flight).
Further down, Blasis is dressed in a toga, a spectator to the mystical scene, and he is surrounded by: Philosophy, Physics, Morality and Mathematics, which lend their assistance to Blasis, who is about to describe what he sees. At the bottom, a *Putto* (representing Human Genius) in the center is flanked to the left by Painting, Sculpture and Poetry, the three sister arts to dance.
For readers who have followed thus far, it will not be very difficult to identify the numerous references to classical iconology and the use of symbology from 18th-Century ballet. Serpents, daggers and clubs, understood as symbols of strength, summon up (respectively) Noverre's *Furies* and *Hercules;* the interpretation of touch or contact as being symbolic of love is reminiscent of the Minuet. The *Putto* in the (lower) center has clear neoclassical origins, while the figure flying above Man and scattering flowers around the world, which represents the *pleasurable passions*, echoes back to the *Hours* by Raphael.
The intent revealed here by Blasis is the cultural education of his students and their introduction to classical iconological tradition.

L' UOMO FISICO, INTELLETTUALE, MORALE

In this table, comprising pages 211, 212 and 213 of *L'Uomo fisico, intellettuale e morale* by Blasis, each of the seventeen images schematically reproduces the overall body positioning in relation to the direction of the gaze. The trajectory of the gaze is envisaged as a single line, so as to demonstrate its fundamental function within the general structure of the figure.

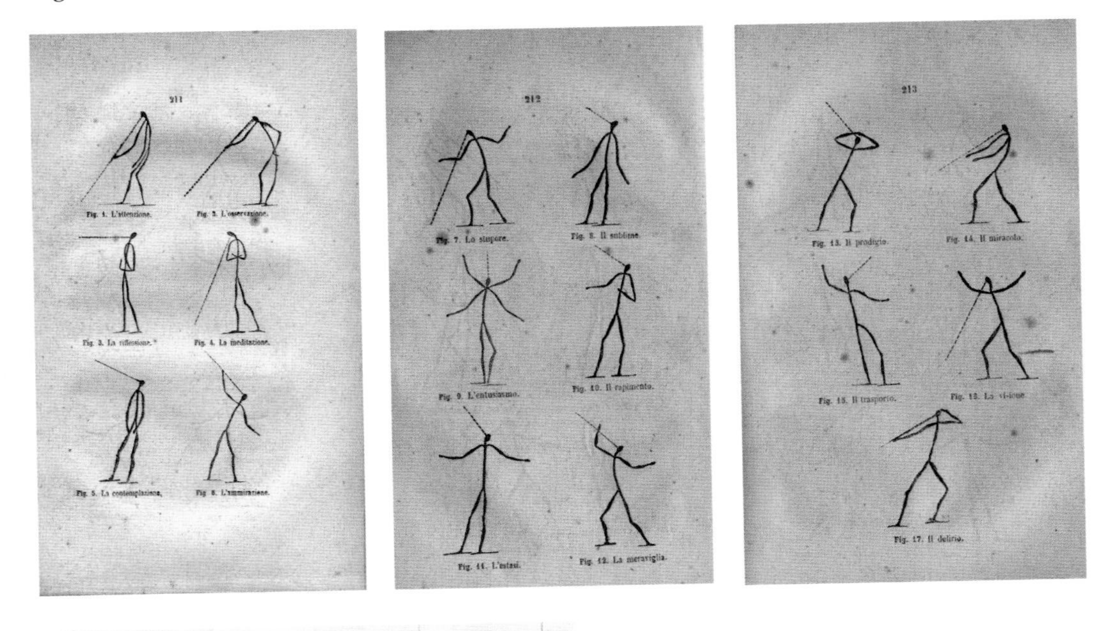

This image to the left, corresponding to Table III of the same book (p. 218), illustrates the "Motions of the soul conceived under the image of the directions of movement of the body. New theory of expression."
The graphic indications superimposed over the figures, as well as the mobility displayed in the figures themselves, emphasize both the tension in a body that is moved by emotion and the significance given to certain aspects and parts of the body (hands, gaze, etc.) in the expression of various states of mind. The body shifts away from verticality and bends or inclines, grading the amount of energy in relation to the emotional state and the intensity of the sentiments (see also pp. 82-85).

By comparing Table IV of Blasis' *L'Uomo fisico, intellettuale e morale* (left) with the table from the 1804 edition of Leonardo da Vinci's *Treatise on Painting* (right), we can demonstrate how Blasis was inspired by the great painter in his representation of the "Theory of the center of gravity". The figures are drawn with simple lines, in order to highlight the position of the "center", and they are organized according to a "rising" order that leads from the elementary state of man (first figure, upper left) to the more elevated and noble aspects of dancing (flying figures, lower right).
Similarity is to be found in the figure of the man who carries a load upon his shoulders, which appears in the second row of both tables, second figure from the left.
This citation by Blasis was intended to confer additional cultural dignity to his creation.

The French and Italian Schools in the Late 19th Century

From French Verisimilitude to Italian Realism

Catarina ou la Fille du bandit, already referred to on page 198, is one of the most renowned works by the choreographer Jules Perrot and also one of the most significant creations from an adventurous streak in French Romantic ballet. After its premiere at Her Majesty's Theatre in London in 1846, the ballet went through such a major reworking for the version presented at La Scala in 1847 that this latter was to become the final, definitive version of the ballet. The success it encountered in Milan set in motion a chain of re-stagings all over Italy, beginning in 1847 and continuing up to and beyond the unification of the nation in 1861. Its warm reception by the Italian public was due to its captivating plot, the dynamism of its scenes and dances, the Italian setting – adventures in the land of Abruzzo, where 17th-Century painter Salvator Rosa is captured by bandits – and, as was usual, to the way in which the production was adapted to the Italian market. The modifications – which differed depending on the version and regarded the dancing, costumes, music and, above all, the mimed sections – were, in any case, so major that, by the time Enrico Cecchetti was engaged to remount the ballet at the Maryinsky Theater in 1888, what the public saw was a performance quite different from the one that had been presented in St. Petersburg in 1849. For the ballet had been "Italian-ized".
In Cecchetti's version, the ballet acquired a dramatic incisiveness and a realism that were far-removed from French Romantic tastes. Dances of Italian origins were added (the Tucicici from Abruzzo and the Dance of the Moccoletti, which was typical of the last day of Carnival in Rome); the manner in which the bandits held their rifles was altered ("Present arms", "Shoulder arms", "Order arms"); popular expressions were inserted, like *Diavolino*'s impudent "shoulder shrug"; and the mimed sections were separated from the dance and developed into broad works in their own right.

In this print, published in 1840 in the scientific periodical *Museo scientifico, letterario ed artistico*, the artist *Salvator Rosa* is painting a portrait of one of the brigands from Abruzzo or Calabria, with the others all around – testimony to a general interest in the subject.

The images on this page and page 198 compare the original French version of Jules Perrot's ballet *Catarina ou la Fille du bandit* with the Italian version of the same ballet, staged by Cecchetti. The figure on p. 198 (lower right) portrays Lucile Grahn with Jules Perrot. On this page, below, two photographs of Enrico Cecchetti in the role of *Diavolino* are accompanied by a print from *Three Months passed in the Mountains East of Rome during the Year 1819*, by Maria Calcott (Maria Graham), which documents the traditional dress and footwear of the Ciociaria, an area that extends between the regions of Lazio, Abruzzo and Molise in central Italy.
The differences between the images on page 198 and those on this page are substantial, and they highlight the contrast between the cultivated interpretation of the peasant world, with its adventurous plots – typical of the French Romantic and late-Romantic ballet – and the realism and descriptive style of Italian dance at the end of the 19th Century. Grahn and Perrot's gestures and also their clothing are the results of traditional characteristics being stylized in a theatrical language. Despite the girl's musket (p. 198, lower left) and the basic features of the costume itself, her attitude reveals nobility, while various charming touches exalt the femininity of the danseuse (the shawl elegantly drawn over her soft tutu, for example, and her rather bonnet-like hat). Similarly, the costume of her lieutenant, Jules Perrot, is very stylized, in keeping with his elegant positioning and the ostentatious technical precision.
The costume worn by Enrico Cecchetti in the two photographs from the Cecchetti family archives – which were retrieved by Livia Brillarelli and are now kept at the Theater Museum at La Scala – has, on the other hand, a simple wide-brimmed hat typical of traditional 19th-Century Abruzzo costumes, with footwear from the traditional Ciociaria costume (*ciocia*), and a shirt and small, tight-fitting jacket.
The authentic eloquence of his pose and the proud gaze both corroborate the realism that was discussed in chronicles of the era, as we also see documented in this lovely illustration from Maria Graham's book.

Technique and Teachings in the Late 19th Century: a Time for Systemization and Reorganization

As we have seen (on pp. 153-158), during the course of the 19th Century, dance technique developed in tandem with the latest aesthetic lines, and also with expectations that ballet be spectacular. In the 1850s – after the great innovations promoted during the late 1700s and early 1800s by the emerging generation of Pierre Gardel and Auguste Vestris, and after the following generation that included Carlo Blasis and August Bournonville as major players – male technique was to suffer an arresting blow, losing its privileged position as "master" of the stage. Arthur Saint-Léon, Ferdinand Hoppe, Lucien Petipa and a handful of others were to be the last flag-bearers of a glorious school of male dancing that was now headed toward extinction – one which, according to Théophile Gautier in *La Presse* (July 25, 1843): "... assumes neither that false grace, nor that ambiguous and revolting winsomeness which have turned the public against male dancing."
The new Romantic plots, in which the female dancer was considered the dramatic mainstay of the adventures, were to give ample space for the advancement of technique in women's dancing, a process that had been already well underway by the end of the 18th Century. After having attained "aerial" technique in the early 1800s – both in jumps and in the lifting of the legs – women were now creating an acrobatic technique all their own: the rise onto the tips of the toes, leaving the development of the *pirouette*, the big jumps and the technique of providing support in the *pas de deux* to the men.
Following on the great school of the Gardels (Maximilien and Pierre), the Vestris' (Gaetano and Auguste) and François Coulon at the Paris Opera, a new generation in France, headed by Albert (François Decombe) and Filippo Taglioni, were to update teaching methods, adapting these to the new stylistic and physical demands. At the same time, Carlo Blasis was at La Scala (1837-1850), restructuring that school and taking it to unsurpassed qualitative levels. This was an extremely important transitional phase for classical dance technique, during which experimentation and the search for novelty was to gradually give way to systemization and reorganization.
Toward the end of the 19th Century, the positions of the arms, the legs and the *arabesques* would be definitively named and classified, and the fixed points of the room (i.e., directions in space) were assigned. At the end of the 1880s, the trend in European, especially Italian, dance was to program the teaching schedule according to the days of the week. Among the various teachers who left evidence to this effect, Enrico Cecchetti stands out as the one who achieved the most complete and rational program.
On the following pages, we have created a table summarizing the positions in *arabesque, croisé* and *effacé* in both the French tradition and the Cecchetti Method. Although this is only a representative sampling, comparison between them provides evidence of both the continuity and the revisionary choices made by the different schools at the end of the century.

The Traditional French Arabesque

One distinctive trait of the original *arabesque* was its innovative mobility of the body, which took the arms into positions that diverged from the canonical positions based on opposition and induced the torso to incline forward, in contravention of the rules of *aplomb*.

This aspect is shown in the print here to the left, which portrays the marble bust dedicated by the students of the Imperial Royal Academy of Dance and Mime in Milan to their *Maestro*, Carlo Blasis, in 1838.
Among the girls immersed in the Romantic clouds that surround the effigy of Blasis, many are seen in *arabesque*, with their torsos bending quite far forward (note the two on the lower left, for example).
A forward inclination of the torso recurs in the *arabesques* of the French School up to and beyond the end of the century.
This trait can also be clearly gathered from certain drawings in Arthur Saint-Léon's *Sténochorégraphie* (1852) and, above all, in Théleur's *Letters on Dancing* (1831), an example from which is placed below, left.

Here below, center and right, the two illustrations from Berthe Bernay's book *La danse au théâtre* (1890) show how, in the Paris Opera's *arabesque* at the end of the century, the body would still provide balance to the leg lifted to the back, and, in its entirety, the figure maintained a visibly horizontal line.

In the first images on this page, the evolution of the *arabesque* in the modern Russian School (Vaganova) is compared with that of the new Italian School (Cecchetti Method). The difference is immediately apparent: in the Russian *arabesques* (female figures, left), the body compensates for the opening of the leg behind by shifting forward; in the drawings by Randolph Schwabe for C. W. Beaumont's book on the Cecchetti Method (male figures, right), on the other hand, the body is perpendicular and over the supporting leg.
In the Cecchetti Method, however, the 4th and 5th *arabesques* are in *demi-plié*, which is why the trunk is shifted forward, providing a counterweight to the leg lifted behind.

As we have seen, in the 18th Century, the term *croisé* derived from the crossing of one leg over the other, while *effacé* related to the pulling back of one shoulder in interactions with a partner (see p. 30: effacer = hiding by retraction). From the evidence left by August Bournonville, it can be gathered how the *effacé* using exclusively the movement of the shoulders was to become a general expression referring to the entire body. The same was to occur with *croisé*, the meaning of which shifted from the (crossed) leg to an orientation of the whole body, in respect to the public. This interpretation was assembled in the Russian School and then by Cecchetti, during his long stay in that country.
Despite sharing the term, however, substantial differences remain between Vaganova and Cecchetti, which can be easily recognized in the figures below. On the left (Vaganova), the side arm is raised to horizontal, and the arm "au dessus de la tête" is effectively above the head, while the shoulders and chest are in decisively oblique positions. In the figure to the right, on the other hand, from the Cecchetti Method, a great affinity to the school of Blasis (see pp. 141-142) can be gathered: the chest tends toward a frontal orientation, and the side arm is placed on a low diagonal, while the other is in approximate correspondence to the shoulder, not above the head.
In conclusion, while Vaganova remained faithful to tradition in her *arabesques*, she followed a modern line as regards the body's placement in *croisé* and *effacé*. In the Cecchetti Method, the opposite occurred.

The Sleeping Beauty: the Fable as Metaphor

The Sleeping Beauty, one of the ballets most representative of production in Russia during the late 19th Century, was born out of the fertile collaboration between the choreographer Marius Petipa, the musician Peter Ilyich Tchaikovsky and the director of the Imperial theaters, Ivan Alexandrovich Vsevolozhsky, who also designed the costumes. The first performance took place on January 3, 1890 at the Maryinsky Theater in St. Petersburg, with Pavel Gerdt in the role of Prince Désiré, the ballerina from La Scala Carlotta Brianza as Aurora, and the virtuoso Enrico Cecchetti in dual roles, as both the evil fairy Carabosse (a mime role *en travesti*) and the Bluebird.
The ballet, consisting of three acts and a prologue, was inspired by the celebrated fable by Charles Perrault published in 1697 in the collection *Tales of Mother Goose*, and it was presented as a sumptuous performance, with a clear design and easily understandable implications of political, moral and pedagogic import. It was a fantastical evocation of the golden age of Louis XIV and his conceptual connection to Czar Alexander III, which was celebrated in a final apotheosis in the "style of antiquity": the apparition of Apollo, in a Louis XIV-style costume, illuminated by the sun and surrounded by fairies.
Although the dramatic framework of the tale is simple (as in the Grimm brothers' *Briar Rose*, the gloomy ending from Perrault's original was eliminated), the structure of the ballet was extremely complex – in its multiplicity of characters and "situations" (to use an expression of Noverre's) and in the extraordinary development of its dances and solos. Many of the "situations" were, in fact, simply pretexts for a multi-colored dance performance. The Prince's arrival at the forest in front of the dormant castle, for example, was developed from entertainment and games (among these, Blind Man's Bluff), to lead the spectator into a teasing, late 18th-Century atmosphere, and toward the moment of the Princess' awakening after the infamous one-hundred-year curse. The marriage ceremony offered a starting point for an exhibition of mimic and technical virtuosity, the most sparkling moment of which was the parade of characters taken both from Perrault's fables – *Little Red Riding Hood, Little Thumbling, Donkey Skin, Cinderella, Puss in Boots and Bluebeard*) – and from the more or less coeval tales by Madame d'Aulnoy (*The Bluebird* and *The White Cat*) and by Madame de Villeneuve (*The Beauty and the Beast*).
For the rest, all of the principal elements from French choreographic tradition are traceable in the ballet: the differentiation of choreographic *genres*, the revelatory dream-vision, the counter-positioning of reality and fantasy, the significance of moral themes and, above all, the contrast between Good and Evil. Further, as had been consolidated through tradition, the fairies (representing good and evil) were introduced by a stylistically-similar dancing "follower": frightening and deformed, in the case of the wicked Carabosse; reassuring and beautiful for the beneficent Lilac Fairy. It is indeed the latter – the lovely, youthful bearer of peace and felicity – who, placed in opposition to the old, ugly and malefic fairy Carabosse, mitigates the spell, enabling Good to triumph.
The ballet's overall design is recognizable in the costumes designed by the same Vsevolozhsky, who drew abundantly from the fascinating visual patrimony provided by illustrations for fables and imaginary tales published in the second half of the

century. But beyond the drawings for *Tales of Mother Goose* by Gustave Doré (Paris, 1861), which the artist had set in a late-Gothic style architectural framework, the costumier Vsevolozhsky appears to have also referred back to the era of Louis XIV. This is demonstrated in the costumes for King Floristan's court during the prologue and also those of the dancing Princes in Act III (note the Bluebird, as well), dressed up in the type of "Roman costume" that had been used in theatrical performances at the end of the 17th Century (see pp. 18, 19, 40 and 214).
The illustrations by J. J. Grandville for *Les Fleurs animées* (here below and on the following page, lower left) – which was splendidly reprinted in 1867 – can be recognized in the costumes for the *Lilac Fairy*, the *Nymphs* and the *Candide Fairy*.
As in the purest tradition of fantastical ballets of mythological or *féerique* (fairy-like) nature, in *The Sleeping Beauty*, the iconographic apparatus still carries out a primary function: that of joining ballet's calling to provide a "pleasure for the eyes" to its obligations as a courier of moral, social and political messages.

On this page are four images that demonstrate how Vzevolozhsky was inspired by certain drawings made by Grandville for *Les Fleurs animées.* Above: the original costume designs for the *Candide Fairy* and *Lilac Fairy*; note the resemblance to the drawing on the preceding page. Below: Grandville's drawing for the *Lilac Flower* (left) and the original costume design for the *Lilac Fairy* in the prologue (right).

Upper left: a drawing attributed to Henri de Gissey for a *ballet de cour* (ca. 1660). Upper right: costume sketch by Vzevolozhsky for *Prince Désiré* (Act III, Scene V). Lower left: Henri de Gissey's costume for *Amour* (Cupid), from the opera *Psyché* by Lully (1671); note the extraordinary similarity to that of *The Bluebird* (lower right). In the figure of the Splendid King, who, imprisoned in the body of a (blue) bird, is in love with the Princess Florina, references to the era of the Sun King are evident in the ostentatious elements: from the shoes with heel and buckle and the short Roman skirt, to the ruff and the diagonal band that crosses his chest.

1660

1890

1671

1890

To conclude this medley of characters, here are three costume sketches by Vzevolozhsky.
Top: the evil fairy *Carabosse* (left) and one of his monstrous pages. The *grotesque* character of the evil witch was portrayed with great dramatic force by Enrico Cecchetti *en travesti*, his body and face deformed, as were his gestures.
Lower left: *Puss in Boots*, from the parade of fable characters from the age of Louis XIV. The costume sketch for the *Puss* reveals Vzevolozhsky's inspiration: the illustrations by Gustave Doré for Perrault's fables (lower right), discussed earlier on page 212. The early 17th-Century costume is shrewdly grafted onto the cat body, leaving space for a *grotesque* characterization, where "grotesque" refers to the character being expressed outside of the academic schemes.

Between Tradition and Modernity: the Historical, Allegorical, Fantastical *Excelsior*

The *gran ballo Excelsior* was the most famous Italian choreographic creation of the 19th Century, and its international resonance was of such proportions that it enjoyed great success not only all across Europe (Paris, London, St. Petersburg, Budapest, Berlin and Vienna, et al), but also in the far reaches of the "New World" (San Francisco, New York, Buenos Aires, Rio de Janeiro, Montevideo and others). It was first staged on January 11, 1881 at La Scala in Milan, where it was presented as a succession of eleven scenes, strung together in six sections, which played out over ca. 90 minutes, without intermission.

Its description as "choreographic, historical, allegorical and fantastical action" summarizes with clarity the character of the ballet, which, in tune with positivist currents, proposed a solemn celebration of technical and scientific progress, which were seen as the carriers of peace, prosperity and an improvement of the human condition. The scientific and technical conquests celebrated by the ballet were two "historic" inventions – the first steamship, by Denis Papin (1707), and the battery, by Alessandro Volta (1799) – and two recently-completed works of high engineering: the building of the Suez Canal (1869) and the Alpine tunnel at Moncenisio (1872). These were the four achievements of man that, as is reaffirmed repeatedly in the transcriptions, had instigated the beneficial coming together of the earth's races and people more than any others. It was from this same perspective that the Abolition of Slavery scene was inserted – "human progress" produced by the victory of Reason (*Light*) over ignorance and violence (*Obscurantism*).

The ballet opened and closed with allegorical scenes. The first brought onto stage, in mimic form, the battle between the *Genius of Evil* (*Obscurantism*) and *Light*, which flowed into the second scene's solemn celebration (in dance) of the victory of *Light*, set at the grandiose, classical-imitation temple of Science and Knowledge. Scene XI praised the concord of nations, with plenty of festive flag-waving, before ending with an apotheosis.

Illustrated table from *Excelsior*, published in the periodical *La Luna* (Turin, 1882, no. 54). The author of the sketches, G. Dalsani (artist's name for Giorgio Ansaldi), highlights in a refined and witty way the ballet's multi-dimensional scenario, in which allegoric figures and characters from the most diverse nationalities and historical periods are mixed together in a picturesque manner.

Symbols and Metaphors in Allegoric Figures from **Excelsior**

After *Excelsior*'s first performance, enthusiastic reviews were published in the press praising not only the originality of the plot, but also the splendid tailoring of the dances. The opening up to a new international language was also discussed, and the tact and measure with which elevated concepts and themes of high moral value were rendered was noted.

The conceptual pillar of the ballet was, as we have seen, world peace, or the concord among peoples and political peace between nations – a peace only attainable through *Civilization*, understood to be the education and instruction of the masses. It is, then, not by chance that *Civilization*, a central character and allegoric figure in the scenes *Light* (II) and *Concord between Nations* (XI), would have symbols imprinted on her costume that allude to the mission assigned to her. In the scene in praise of Science and Knowledge (*Light*), letters of the alphabet and numbers appear on the upper part of her bodice, clear references to the schooling of the population. In the final scene, *Concord between Nations*, flags of the various nations are lined up on the upper edge of her bodice, on a short vest made with the national flag of the country in which the ballet was being performed. A similar choice is encountered in the scene in praise of the building of the Suez Canal: *Civilization* has the word *Pax* (Peace) printed on her bodice.

In the photos below: La Scala prima ballerina Adele Besesti, as *Civilization* during spring season, 1881, in the scenes entitled *Light* and *The Suez Canal*, respectively.

Between Verisimilitude and Philology: the "Historical" Context of **Excelsior**

Attention to historical and contextual precision was already growing during the heart of the Romantic era, as the approximation that had greatly characterized productions from the first half of the century began to give way to an attitude of respect toward the text of a ballet, progressively leaning toward a realism that, in some cases, aimed at philological reconstruction.
Documentary precision is one of the positive verdicts aimed at Alfredo Edel, costume designer for the *gran ballo Excelsior* and one of the most interesting interpreters of positivism in ballet. And precision certainly is one of the characteristics specific to Scene III, entitled *The First Steamship*, which recalls the painful story of Denis Papin, whose ship was destroyed by local boatmen incited by the Genius of Evil. For this scene, Edel dedicated himself to meticulous documentary research, the results of which are easily recognizable in the images on this and the following pages, which compare Edel's costume sketches to traditional costumes from Germany (Baden and Alsace), taken from the already-cited publication by Braun & Schneider (1861-1880). On the left, costume sketches from the collection of the La Scala Theater Foundation are arranged; on the right, traditional costumes. The characters portrayed here are, in order: *Kunegonda*, mother of the boatman Valentino; Valentino's fiancée, *Fanny*; and *Valentino* himself.

Costume sketch by Edel for *Kunegonda*
(Property of Fondazione Teatro alla Scala di Milano)

Traditional 19th-Century German costumes

Costume sketch by Edel
for *Fanny*
(Property of Fondazione
Teatro alla Scala di Milano)

Traditional 19th-Century German costumes

Costume sketch by Edel
for *Valentino*
(Property of Fondazione Teatro
alla Scala di Milano)

Traditional 19th-Century German costumes

Caramba's New Excelsior

After more than twenty years of performances and reprises, a new version of *Excelsior* took to the stage on December 30, 1908. Signing the revisions of the stage design and costumes was Caramba (artist's name for Luigi Sapelli), who was very much in vogue at the time for his intelligent and original creations.
Caramba's approach to the scenes from *Excelsior* that we have already examined is decidedly different. Accentuating the allegoric and fantastical elements, he counters Edel's precision with a freer vision, which, without renouncing the documentary aspect, allows more space for fantasy and a more dynamic use of color.
Observing Caramba's costume sketches of the *Allegories*, from the collection of the Fondazione Cassa di Risparmio di Alessandria, we see that in Caramba's versions, symbols in praise of glory and peace are superimposed in an emphatic manner onto the costumes for *Fame* and *Concord* from Scene II, *Light*. But the crown of bay, the wings of Victory, the hearts, and the doves inscribed with "Pax" all have functions that are not only symbolic, inasmuch as they have actually become structural elements.

Caramba's costume for *Light* (below, right) was inspired by a model for an evening dress that had just been launched by Mariano Fortuny, while the costume for *Obscurantism* was loaded with symbols that recollect ignorance (the ear and donkey's tail) and darkness (bat wings).

A similar formulation can be seen in the costumes for the allegories *Electric Light* and the *Telegraph* from Scene IV, which praises the progress resulting from Alessandro Volta's invention of the battery. *Electric Light* has a lampshade on her head and is humorously given *appliqués* to hold that celebrate the installation of light in private homes. Swallows and wires are playfully wrapped around the allegory of the *Telegraph*, who has wheels and sparks on her head.

Observing the "historical" costumes for Scene III from *Excelsior*, set in Germany in 1707, we see that, in contrast to Edel, Caramba takes traditional Swiss costumes as inspiration, re-working these with great vivacity and wit. Color is regarded with modern taste (note the showy floral decorations), and the apron, which had until this time remained the symbol *par excellence* for traditional-national costumes, has indeed now disappeared.
Here in the upper figures, Caramba's *Peasants* are compared with the female character from Filippo Taglioni's ballet *Nathalie, ou la Laitière Suisse* (Paris Opera, 1832), to identify both Caramba's references to traditional costumes (the small lace bonnet, for example) and the gulf between these and his own.
In the lower figures, a comparison between Caramba's *Boatman* and traditional late 18th-Century costumes from Switzerland – reproduced here from the cited publication by Braun & Schneider – underlines the analogies between the two, as well as the interpretive freedom.

Costume sketches by Caramba for the *Contadinelle del Weser* (Peasants from the Weser)

Nathalie, 1832

Costume sketch by Caramba for *Battelliere* (Boatman)

Late 18th-Century Swiss costumes

From Stage to Screen: Luca Comerio's *Excelsior*

After its premiere on January 11, 1881 and the 103 performances given during that same year, the *gran ballo Excelsior* remained on the playbills in Milan, between La Scala and the Canobbiana Theater, for more than twenty years, while simultaneously touring the world, enjoying enormous success all the while.
In the early 1900s, when interest in *Excelsior* appeared to be waning, a new version for the 1908/09 season, directed by the renowned costume designer Caramba (Luigi Sapelli), returned public attention to Manzotti's masterpiece.
Its success, despite the concomitant and disastrous earthquake in Messina, was again so extraordinary that in 1913, film director Luca Comerio decided to transpose the ballet onto film. This is how *Excelsior*'s extraordinary cinematic adventure was born. And despite the fragility of the inflammable film, it has managed to survive, thanks to a fortunate combination of events, even if only in a small fragment that contains the first two allegoric scenes from the ballet: *Obscurantism* and *Light*.
This fragment, property of the Italian National Cineteca, has been restored in different stages, and sound has also been integrated, in a joint operation executed by the author, together with a team of dance experts and technicians from the Cineteca.
From this fragment, we selected a series of images from Scene I that testify in an extremely suggestive manner to the dialogue between the allegories for *Bene-Luce* (Good-Light) and *Male-Oscurantismo* (Evil-Obscurantism), and to the Italian mimic style at the end of the 19th Century. Two frames from the film documenting alterations in film tone – blue for the night effect and red for fire – are reprinted on page 231.

Before moving on to the analysis of the film images, observe this postcard from 1914, displaying the *tableau vivant* that opens Scene II, in which the victory of Science and Knowledge is extolled. The scenery represents the Temple of Light. On the "curvature of the world" (a curved practicable), the symbolic encounter of the allegories *Light* and *Civilization* is portrayed. At stage level, we see the army of the allegories in formation. At the center, on one knee, is *Fame*; at her sides, *Concord* (light-colored costume) and *Invention* (dark-colored costume). Golden lions with symbols of Strength line the sides of the main stage; at the base of the curvature of the world are the *Trumpeters of Fame*, in the act of sounding the melody that precedes the solemn oath. *Obscurantism*, stunned, is about to rise and flee.

The images from Scene I, reprinted on this and the following pages, are from the Film Archives at the National Cineteca in Rome and have been re-worked from the original film frames.
The scene takes place in a desolate setting, among the smoldering ruins of an imaginary Spain during the era of the Inquisition. *Light* is sitting at the feet of *Obscurantism*, lifeless, while the latter boasts of his destructive powers. But a miraculous ray appears together with a soft melody, a sign of heavenly intervention, reawakening *Light*, who recovers her role as messenger of divine will and dispenser of joy and well-being. *Obscurantism* abandons his dominant attitude, assuming miserable and twisted positions, before making one final, desperate attempt to combat *Light*, only to be cursed and punished instead, while the "marvelous" Temple of Light and Knowledge appears, as if in a dream.

Procession of monks,
Spanish soldiers and
prisoners.
Obscurantism points to
the Light...

... which had, at first,
dominated the world...

... and now lay at its feet.

Reawakening, Light moves toward the divine ray.

Kisses of thanks Obscurantism in a by-play: his body is contorted in a wretched manner.

Gestures of joy.

Gesture of threat.

"It is God's will."

Obliging Obscurantism into an attitude of submission.

"You" [and these ruins]

"... are damned."

Rebellious reaction by Obscurantism to the gesture "It is God's will."

Luca Comerio's film of *Excelsior* (1913); Scene I, *Obscurantism*. Film Archives of the Cineteca Nazionale, Rome.
The scene begins. Standing above the ruins, the Genius of *Darkness* indicates with satisfaction the prostration of *Light*, which has been defeated by Evil.
Light is wearing the new dress conceived by Caramba (see p. 221, upper right), while *Obscurantism* wears the costume originally designed by Alfredo Edel (see p. 216).

Luca Comerio's film of *Excelsior* (1913); Scene I, *Obscurantism*. Film Archives of the Cineteca Nazionale, Rome.
These two single frames of film are from the final moment of the battle between *Light* and *Obscurantism*, which culminates in the victory of Good, amidst frightening flashes of fire.
The different colors of the frames are evidence of the technique of toning (film coloration), commonly used in silent movies. By convention, the color blue indicates a nocturnal atmosphere. Red is used, in this case, to accentuate the dramatic power of the moment and to create a strong contrast with the following scene, which is a hymn to Knowledge and Science, the fruits of divine will.

Bibliographical References

Books cited in the text

Antichità di Ercolano, Le, 9 vols, Nella Regia Stamperia, Naples, 1755-92.

Batteux, Charles, *Les Beaux-Arts réduits à un même principe*, Durand, Paris, 1746.

Beaumont, Cyril W. Idzikowski, Stanislas, *A Manual of the Theory and Practice of Classical Theatrical Dancing*, illustr. Randolph Schwabe, C. W. Beaumont, London, 1922.

Berchoux, Joseph, *La Danse, ou les Dieux de l'Opéra. Poëme en VI chants*, Giguet et Michaud, Paris, 1806.

Bernay, Berthe, *La danse au théâtre*, E. Dentu, Paris, 1890.

Blasis, Carlo, *L'Uomo fisico, intellettuale e morale, opera di Carlo De Blasis*, Tipografia Guglielmini, Milan, 1857; 2nd ed. Tipografia dir. Gernia, Milan, 1868 (facsimile ed. Ornella Di Tondo and Flavia Pappacena, LIM, Lucca, 2005 [2007]).

Blasis, Carlo, *Manuel complet de la danse, comprenant la théorie, la pratique et l'histoire de cet art depuis les temps les plus reculés jusqu'a nos jours, trad. de l'anglais de M. Barton, sur l'edit. de 1830 par M. Paul Vergnaud, et revu par M. Gardel*, Librairie Encyclopédique de Roret, Paris, 1830 (facsimile Leonce Laget, Paris, 1980).

Blasis, Carlo, *Mefistofele, ossia Il genio del male, ballo poetico-filosofico in nove quadri, La Fama*, 1843: Mar. 23, 30; Apr. 6, 10, 20, 24; May 1.

Blasis, Carlo, *The Code of Terpsichore: a Practical and Historical Treatise on the Ballet, Dancing, and Pantomime; with a Complete Theory of the Art of Dancing*, transl. R. Barton, James Bulcock, London, 1828 (facsimile Dance Horizons, New York, 1976).

Blasis, Carlo, *Traité élémentaire, théorique et pratique de l'Art de la danse contenant les développemens, et les démonstrations des principes généraux et particuliers, qui doivent guider le danseur*, Joseph Beati et Antoine Tenenti, Milan, 1820 (facsimile Forni, Bologna, 1969; repr. *Traité de l'Art de la Danse*, ed. Flavia Pappacena, Gremese, Rome, 2007; Eng. transl.: *An Elementary Treatise upon the Theory and Practice of the Art of Dancing*, Dover, New York, 1968).

Bon genre, Le, Librairie Denis, Paris, 1810.

Borelli, Giovanni, *De Motu Animalium*, 2 vols, Lugduni in Batavis: apud Johannem de Vivie, Cornelium Boutesteyn, Danielem a Gaesbeeck, & Petrum vander Aa, 1685 (Eng. transl. *On the Movement of Animals*, Springer-Verlag, Berlin-Heidelberg, 1989).

Braun & Schneider, *Zur Geschichte der Kostüme*, Munich, 1861-80.

Brillarelli, Livia (ed.), *Foto d'Archivio. I Cecchetti, una dinastia di ballerini*, Fototeca Comunale, Civitanova Marche, 1992.

Cahusac, Louis de, *La Danse Ancienne et Moderne ou Traité Historique de la Danse*, 3 vols, Jean Neaulme, La Haye, 1754 (repr. Desjonqueres, Paris, 2004).

Campardon, Émile, *Les Spectacles de la foire*, 2 vols, Berger-Levrault, Paris, 1877.

De Boigne, Charles, *Petits mémoires de l'Opéra*, Librairie Nouvelle, Paris, 1857.

De Jaucourt, Louis, *Peinture arabesque ancienne*, in Diderot, Denis – d'Alembert, Jean-Baptiste Le Rond (eds), *Encyclopédie ou Dictionnaire raisonné des sciences des Arts et des Métiers*, vol. XII, 1765, p. 277.

Delord, Taxile, *Les Fleurs animées par J.-J. Grandville*; introd. by Alphonse Karr; text by Taxile Delord, G. de Gonet, Paris, 1847; 2nd ed. Karr, Alphonse and Delord, Taxile and le Comte Fœlix, *Les Fleurs animées, illustrées par Grandville, Nouvelle édition avec planches très soigneusement retouchées pour la gravure et le coloris par M. Louis Joseph Édouard Maubert*, Garnier Frères, Paris, 1867.

De Pure, Michel, *Idée des Spectacles anciens et nouveaux*, Michel Brunet, Paris, 1668 (facsimile Minkoff, Geneva, 1972).

Desboulmiers, Jean-Augustin-Julien, *Histoire du théâtre de l'Opéra comique*, 2 vols, Lacombe, Paris, 1769.

Diderot, Denis and d'Alembert, Jean-Baptiste Le Rond (eds), *Encyclopédie ou Dictionnaire raisonné des sciences des Arts et des Métiers*, Le Breton, 1751-80 (facsimile Friedrich Frommann Verlag, Stuttgart, Bad Cannstatt, 1967).

Donatone, Guido, *William Hamilton. Diario segreto napoletano (1764-1789)*, Grimaldi, Naples, 2000.

Doré, Gustave, *Contes de ma mère l'Oye*, Pierre-Jules Hetzel, Paris, 1861.

Dramaturgija Baleta, Leningrad, 1942.

Du Fresnoy, Charles-Alphonse, *L'Arte della pittura di Carlo Alfonso Du Fresnoy Accresciuta con più recenti e necessarie osservazioni ed arricchita con più Rami, opera molto utile agli Studiosi di Pittura e Scoltura*, A spese di Giuseppe Monti Risecco, Rome, 1775 (facsimile Forni, Sala bolognese, 1981).

Favart, A. P. C., *Mémoires et correspondance littéraires, dramatiques et anecdotiques de C.S. Favart publiés par A.P.C. Favart, son petit-fils, et précédés d'une notice historique rédigée sur pièces authentiques et originales par H.F. Dumoulard*, Léopold Collin, Paris, 1808.

Feuillet, Raoul Auger, *Chorégraphie, ou l'art de décrire la dance par caractères, figures et signes demonstratifs*, Chez l'Auteur, Paris, 1700 (facsimile Forni, Sala bolognese, 1983).

Feuillet, Raoul Auger, *Recueil de Dances contenant un grand nombres des meilleures Entrées de Ballet de M*[r] *Pecour*, Chez le Sieur Feüillet, Paris, 1704 (facsimile Gregg International, 1972).

Gallini, Giovanni-Andrea, *A Treatise on the Art of Dancing*, Dodsley, London, 1762 (facsimile Broude Brothers, New York, 1967).

Gautier, Théophile, *Opéra: La Péri. La Péri, ballet fantastique en 2 acts, sc. Gautier, ch. J. Coralli, mus. Burgmüller, f.p. July 17th 1843, La Presse*, July 25, 1843, in Théophile Gautier, *Gautier on dance*, ed. by Ivor Guest, Dance Books, London, 1986, pp. 112-121.

Gautier, Théophile and Janin, Jules Gabriel and Chasles, Philarète, *Les Beautés de L'Opera, ou Chefs-d'Oeuvre Lyriques*, Soulie, Paris, 1845.

Goya y Lucientes, Francisco, *Caprichos*, 1799.

Graham, Maria, *Three Months Passed in the Mountains East of Rome during the Year 1819*, Longman, Hurst, Rees, Orme, & Brown, London, 1820.

Grimm, Jacob and Wilhelm, *The Fairy Tales of the Brothers Grimm*, Daniel, Noel (eds), Price, Matthew r. (con.), Taschen America, 2011.

Guillaume, *Caractères de la danse Allemande*, Chez l'Auteur, Paris, n.d. [1769].

Hogarth, William, *The Analysis of Beauty*, London, 1753.

Illustrierte Zeitung, Leipzig, 1844, no. 27.

Lambranzi, Gregorio, *Neue und curieuse theatrialische Tantz-Schul*, Nuremberg, 1716 (Eng. transl. *New and Curious School of Theatrical Dancing*, transl. Derra de Moroda, ed. C. W. Beaumont, The Imperial Society of Teachers of Dancing, London, 1928; facsimile Dance Horizons, New York, 1972).

Leonardo da Vinci, *Trattato della pittura*, Società Tipografica de' Classici Italiani, Milan, 1804.

Luna, La, no. 54, Turin, 1882.

Magri, Gennaro, *Trattato teorico-prattico di ballo*, Orsino, Naples, 1779 (repr. *Theoretical and*

Practical Treatise on Dancing, ed. Irmgard E. Berry and Annalisa Fox; transl. Mary Skeaping, with Anna Ivanova and Irmgard E. Berry, Dance Books, London, 1988).

Méreau, Charles-Hubert, *Réflexions sur le maintien et sur les moyens d'en corriger les défauts*, Mevius et Dieterich, Gotha, 1760.

Milizia, Francesco, *Dizionario delle Belle Arti del disegno estratto in gran parte dalla Enciclopedia metodica*, 2 vols, Remondini, Bassano, 1797.

Morrocchesi, Antonio, *Lezioni di Declamazione e d'arte teatrale*, Tipografia all'Insegna di Dante, Florence, 1832 (facsimile Gremese, Rome, 1991).

Museo scientifico, letterario ed artistico, ovvero scelta raccolta di utili e svariate nozioni in fatto di scienze, lettere ed arti belle. Opera compilata da illustri scrittori, Stabilimento Tipografico di Alessandro Fontana, Turin, year II, 1840.

Noverre, Jean-Georges, *Habits de Costume pour l'exécution des Ballets de Mr Noverre dessinés par M. Boquet Dessinateur des menus plaisirs du Roi de France; Habits de Costume pour différents caractères de Danse, d'opéra, de comédie, tragédie et de bal dessinés par M. Boquet Dessinateur des menus plaisirs du Roi de France*, Ludwigsburg, November 10, 1766, vols VII-XI, ms, University of Warsaw Library.

Noverre, Jean-Georges, *Habits de Costume pour l'exécution des Ballets de Mr Noverre dessinés par Mr Boquet Dessinateur des menus Plaisirs du Roi de France*, Paris, January 20, 1791, vol. II, ms, National Library of Sweden.

Noverre, Jean-Georges, *Lettres sur la Danse et sur les Ballets*, Aimé Delaroche, Lyon/Stuttgart, 1760 (facsimile Broude Bros., New York, 1967).

Noverre, Jean-Georges, *Lettres sur la Danse, sur les Ballets et les Arts*, Jean Charles Schnoor, St. Petersburg, 1803-04 (facsimile of Vol. I, ed. Flavia Pappacena, LIM, Lucca, 2011; Eng. transl. of Vol. I, *Letters on Dancing and Ballets*, transl. Cyril W. Beaumont, Beaumont, London, 1930; reprod. New York, Dance Horizons 1966, 1968, 1975; Dance Books, Alton, 2004).

Parfaict, Claude and François, *Dictionnaire des théâtres de Paris*, 7 vols, Rozet, Paris, 1767.

Peter, Frank-Manuel (ed.), *Giselle ou les Willis Ballet Fantastique en deux actes*, Deutsches Tanzarchiv Köln, Georg Olms Verlag, Hildesheim, 2008.

Petit Courrier des Dames, Au Bureau de *Courrier des Dames*, Paris, 1829.

Presse, La, July 25, 1843.

Rameau, Pierre, *Abbregé de la nouvelle méthode dans l'art d'écrire ou de traçer toutes sortes de danses de ville*, Paris, 1725 (facsimile Gregg International, 1972).

Rameau, Pierre, *Le Maître à danser*, Jean Villette, Paris, 1725 (facsimile Broude Bros., New York 1967; 2nd Eng. transl. *The Dancing master; or The Art of Dancing Explained*, transl. John Essex, London, 1731).

Ripa, Cesare, *Iconologia*, Padova, 1618 (reprod. Tea, Milan, 1992).

Saint-Léon, Arthur, *La Sténochorégraphie*, Chez l'Auteur et chez Brandus, Paris (facsimile ed. Flavia Pappacena, LIM, Lucca, 2006).

Saint-Non, Richard de, *Voyage pittoresque ou description des Royaumes de Naples et de Sicile*, 5 vols, Clousier, Paris, 1781-86.

Teatro illustrato e la musica popolare, Il, year VI, no. 62 , Feb., 1886, Special Supplement, Edoardo Sonzogno, Milan, 1886.

Théleur, E. A., *Letters on Dancing*, Sherwood & Co., London, 1831 (facsimile in *Studies in Dance History*, vol. II, No. 1, Fall/Winter, 1990, Introd. Sandra N. Hammond).

Thomas, Antoine Jean-Baptiste, *Un an à Rome et dans ses environs. Recueil de dessins lithographiés, dessiné et public par Thomas*, Firmin Didot, Paris, 1823.

Tomlinson, Kellom, *The Art of Dancing Explained by Reading and Figures*, printed for the author, London, 1735 (facsimile Gregg International / Dance Horizons, 1970).
Vaganova, Agrippina, *Osnovy Klassicheskogo Tantsa*, Iskusstvo, Leningrad, 1934 (Eng. transl. Dover, New York, 1969).
Vaillat, Léandre, *La Taglioni ou La vie d'une danseuse*, Albin Michel, Paris, 1942.
Watelet, Claude-Henri, *Grotesques*, in Diderot, Denis – d'Alembert, Jean-Baptiste Le Rond (eds), *Encyclopédie ou Dictionnaire raisonné des sciences des Arts et des Métiers*, vol. VII, 1757, pp. 966-967.
Weaver, John, *Anatomical and Mechanical Lectures upon Dancing*, London, 1721 (facsimile in Richard Ralph, *The Life and Works of John Weaver*, Dance Books, London, 1985, pp. 861-1031).
Weaver, John, *The Fable of Orpheus and Eurydice*, London, 1718 (facsimile in Richard Ralph, *The Life and Works of John Weaver*, Dance Books, London, 1985, pp. 763-812).
Weaver, John, *The Loves of Mars and Venus*, London, 1717 (facsimile in Richard Ralph, *The Life and Works of John Weaver*, Dance Books, London, 1985, pp. 733-762).

Texts used for iconographic documentation

Dance

Beaumont, Cyril W., *Ballet Design: Past and Present*, The Studio, London, 1946.
Beaumont, Cyril W., *Five Centuries of Ballet Design*, The Studio, London, 1939.
Beaussant, Philippe, *Lully ou Le musicien du Soleil*, Gallimard/Théâtre des Champs-Élysées, Paris, 1992.
Bernay, Berthe, *La danse au théâtre*, E. Dentu, Paris, 1890.
Binney, Edwin 3rd, *Glories of the Romantic Ballet*, Dance Books, London, 1983.
Blok, Lyubov, *Klassichesky Tanets, Istoria i Sovremennost* [Classical Dance, History and Modernity]. Iskusstvo, Moscow, 1987.
Calendoli, Giovanni, *Storia universale della danza*, Mondadori, Milan, 1985.
Carrieri, Raffaele, *La danza in Italia 1500-1900*, Editoriale Domus, Milan, 1949.
Crespi Morbio, Vittoria, *...Guarnizioni spiccantissime. Figurini e schemi coreografici per la rappresentazione del ballo Excelsior all'Eden di Parigi – 1883*, Exhibition Catalogue, Teatro alla Scala, Oct.-Dec., 1993, Edizioni Amici della Scala, Milan, 1993.
Guest, Ivor, *The Ballet of the Enlightenment. The Establishment of the Ballet d'Action in France 1770-1793*, Dance Books, London, 1996.
Guest, Ivor, *Ballet under Napoleon*, Dance Books, London, 2002.
Guest, Ivor, *The Romantic Ballet in Paris*, Dance Books, London, 1980.
Haskell, Arnold, *A Picture History of Ballet*, Hulton Press, London, 1954.
Konstantinova, Marina, *Spiashchaya Krasavitsa. Shedevry Baleta*, Iskusstvo, Moscow, 1990.
Migel, Parmenia, *Great Ballet Prints of the Romantic Era*, Dover, New York, 1981.
Moore, Lilian, *Images of the Dance. Historical Treasures of the Dance Collection 1581-1861*, New York Public Library, New York, 1965.
Pappacena, Flavia (ed.), *Excelsior. Documenti e saggi. Documents and Essays*, Chorégraphie, Scuola Nazionale di Cinema-Cineteca Nazionale, Di Giacomo, Rome, 1998.
Rand, Richard (ed.), *Intimate Encounters, Love and Domesticity in Eighteenth-Century France*, Hood Museum of Art, Dartmouth College, Hanover (N.H.); Princeton University Press, Princeton (N.J.) 1997

Reade, Brian, *Ballet Designs and Illustrations 1581-1940, A Catalogue Raisonné*, Victoria and Albert Museum, Her Majesty's Stationery Office, London, 1967.
Sowell, Madison and Debra and Falcone, Francesca and Veroli, Patrizia, *Il Balletto romantico. Tesori della collezione Sowell*, L'Epos, Palermo, 2007.
Winter, Marian Hannah, *The Pre-Romantic Ballet*, Pitman, London, 1974.

Art and Costumes

Adams, Yvonne, *Meissen Figures 1730-1775 The Kaendler Period*, Schiffer Publishing, Atglen, Pennsylvania, 2001.
Barilli, Renato (ed.), *Canova e Appiani. Alle origini della contemporaneità*, Mazzotta, Milan, 1999.
Bailey, Colin B. (ed.), *The Age of Watteau, Chardin and Fragonard: Masterpieces of French Genre Painting*, Yale University Press, New Haven, in association with the National Gallery of Canada, 2003.
Barroero Liliana, *Il neoclassicismo in Italia. Da Tiepolo a Canova*, Skira, 2002.
Bernini-Pezzini, Grazia and Massari, Stefania and Prosperi-Valenti-Rodinò, Simonetta (eds), *Raphæl invenit. Stampe da Raffaello nelle collezioni dell'Istituto Nazionale per la Grafica*, Ministero per i Beni culturali e ambientali, Istituto Nazionale per la Grafica, Edizioni Quasar, Rome, 1985.
Choné, Paulette and Moureau, François and Quettier, Philippe and Varnier, Éric, *Claude Gillot, 1673-1722: comédies, sabbats et autres sujets bizarres*, Musée de Langres-Somogy, Paris, 1999.
Coutts, Howard, *The Art of Ceramics. European Ceramic Design 1500-1830*, Yale University Press, New Haven, 2001.
Dacos, Nicole, *Le logge di Raffaello. Maestro e bottega di fronte all'antico*, Istituto Poligrafico e Zecca dello Stato, Libreria dello Stato, Rome, 1986.
Flach, Hans Dieter, *Ludwigsburg Porcelain. Fayence, Steingut, Kacheln, Fliesen*, Arnoldsche, Stuttgart, 1997, 2nd ed. 2008.
Gruber, Alain (ed.), *The History of Decorative Arts. Classicism and the Baroque in Europe*, Abbeville Press Publishers, New York, 1996.
Jansen, Reinhard, *Commedia dell'arte. Fest der Komödianten*, Arnoldsche, Stuttgart, 2011.
Jansen, Reinhard, *Dazzling Rococo: Ludwigsburg Porcelain from the Jansen Collection*, Arnoldsche, Stuttgart, 2008.
Pezzini-Bernini, Grazia and Fiorani, Fabio, *Canova e l'incisione*, Ghedina e Tassotti, Bassano del Grappa, 1993.
Pinot de Villechenon, Marie-Noëlle and Napoleone, Caterina, *Ercolano e Pompei. Gli affreschi nelle illustrazioni neoclassiche dell'album delle "Peintures d'Herculanum" conservato al Louvre*, Franco Maria Ricci, Milan, 2000.
Populus, Bernard, *Claude Gillot, 1673-1722, Catalogue de l'œuvre gravé*, Publication de la Société pour l'étude de la gravure française, Paris, 1930.
Rand, Richard (ed.), *Intimate Encounters, Love and Domesticity in Eighteenth-Century France*, Hood Museum of Art, Dartmouth College, Hanover (N.H.); Princeton University Press, Princeton (N.J.), 1997.
Ribeiro, Aileen, *The Art of Dress. Fashion in England and France 1750 to 1820*, Yale University Press, New Haven, 1997.
Stefani, Ottorino, *Canova e l'incisione, I rilievi del Canova*, Electa, Milan, 1990.

Iconographic References

Collections and Public Archives

Archivio Film della Cineteca Nazionale, Rome, pp. 225-231.
Bibliothèque de l'Institut de France, Paris, pp. 19 (top), 42, 43.
Bibliothèque de l'Opéra, Paris, pp. 111, 122, 156 (left), 164 (upper left; bottom), 165.
Bibliothèque Nationale, Paris, pp. 29 (right), 36, 40-41, 45, 46, 123, 129 (top).
Collection of the St Petersburg State Theatre Library, pp. 213 (top; lower right), 214 (upper and lower right), 215 (top; lower left).
Derra de Moroda Dance Archives, Salzburg, pp. 68-71, 145 (left), 147 (upper right).
Deutsches Tanzarchiv Köln, pp. 185-188.
Fondazione Cassa di Risparmio di Alessandria, pp. 220, 221, 222 (upper left and center; lower left), cover photo.
Fondazione Teatro alla Scala di Milano, Archivio Storico bozzetti e figurini, pp. 218 (left), 219 (left).
Museo-Biblioteca Teatrale alla Scala, Milan, pp. 192-194, 199, 200, 207 (lower right and center), 209 (upper left), 217.
National Library of Sweden / Kungliga Biblioteket, pp. 100 (right), 103 (right), 108, 109 (top), 110, 114, 115-119 (right), 120, 170 (upper right; bottom), 173 (lower left).
The University of Warsaw Library: Photo: The Print Room of the University of Warsaw Library: Zb.król.vol.801-805), pp. 78, 79, 92, 96, 97 (upper; lower left), 98 (top), 99, 100 (left), 101, 102, 103 (left), 104-107, 115-119 (left), 170 (upper left), 172.

Museums

Art Institute of Chicago, p. 74.
Boston Museum of Fine Arts, Forsyth Wickes Bequest, p. 82.
Casa del Canova, Possagno, p. 139.
Detroit Institute of Arts (Michigan), p. 131.
Fowler McCormick Collection, Chicago, p. 127.
Galleria degli Uffizi, Florence, p. 25 (lower right).
Historisches Museum Basel, Pauls-Eisenbeiss-Stiftung, p. 86.
Hofburg (Schloss Schönbrunn), Vienna, p. 126.
Kunstmuseum Luzern, p. 197 (lower right).
Musée Carnavalet, Paris, p. 167.
Musée Cognacq-Jay, Paris, p. 113 (upper right).
Musée de l'Opéra, Paris, p. 44, 53 (bottom), 88, 161, 164, 174.
Musée des Beaux-Arts di Besançon, p. 93.
Musée des Beaux-Arts de Dijon, p. 128 (bottom).
Musée du Louvre, pp. 19 (bottom), 129 (A. Dequier - M. Bard; bottom), 136 (bottom), 137 (left), 138, 164 (right), 174.
Musée National de Malmaison, Paris, pp. 136 (top), 140.

Musée National du Château, Fontainebleau, p. 113.
Musei Vaticani, Rome, p. 25.
Museo di Capodimonte, p. 137 (right).
National Gallery of Scotland, Edinburgh, p. 48.
National Museum, Stockholm, p. 214 (lower left).
Nelson-Atkins Museum of Art, Kansas City (Missouri), p. 49.
Palazzo Pitti, Florence, p. 29.
Residenzschloss, Ludwigsburg, pp. 37, 77 (left), 125, 161.
Stiffung Preussische Schlösser und Gärten Berlin-Brandenburg, p. 60.
Tate Gallery, London, p. 62.
Toledo Museum of Art (Ohio), p. 112.
Victoria and Albert Museum, London, pp. 18, 214.

Private Collections

Allen Charles Klein Collection, p. 207.
F. Pappacena Collection, pp. 66, 76 (bottom), 109, 124, 132, 134, 139 (bottom), 141, 142, 144 (bottom), 146 (top), 147 (upper left), 149-150, 151 (top), 155, 156 (right), 157, 161 (right), 166 (right), 167 (left), 168, 171 (bottom), 175, 176, 178-183, 190, 195, 197 (top, lower left), 198 (top), 202-204, 206, 207 (top), 209 (bottom), 210, 212, 213 (lower left), 215 (lower right), 218 (right), 219 (right), 222 (lower right), 223, 224.
D. M. Sowell Collection, pp. 166 (left), 173 (top; lower right), 189, 198 (bottom), 222 (upper right).
L. Tanca Collection, pp. 35, 94, 113 (lower left), 152.

Where not indicated in the text, the images are from other private collections.
For images from texts re-published in facsimile, please refer to the bibliography.